Your
Horoscope
2022

. . . .

Scorpio

24 October – 22 November

igloobooks

igloobooks

Published in 2021
First published in the UK by Igloo Books Ltd
An imprint of Igloo Books Ltd
Cottage Farm, NN6 0BJ, UK
Owned by Bonnier Books
Sveavägen 56, Stockholm, Sweden
www.igloobooks.com

0721 001
2 4 6 8 10 9 7 5 3 1
ISBN 978-1-80022-528-2

Written by Belinda Campbell and Denise Evans

Designed by Simon Parker
Edited by Suzanne Fossey

Printed and manufactured in China

CONTENTS

....

INTRODUCTION
· · · · · · · · · · · · · · · · ·

This 15-month guide has been designed and written to give
a concise and accessible insight into both the nature of your
star sign and the year ahead. Divided into two main sections,
the first section of this guide will give you an overview of your
character in order to help you understand how you think,
perceive the world and interact with others and – perhaps just
as importantly – why. You'll soon see that your zodiac sign
is not just affected by a few stars in the sky, but by planets,
elements, and a whole host of other factors, too.

The second section of this guide is made up of daily forecasts.
Use these to increase your awareness of what might appear on
your horizon so that you're better equipped to deal with the
days ahead. While this should never be used to dictate your
life, it can be useful to see how your energies might be affected
or influenced, which in turn can help you prepare for what life
might throw your way.

By the end of these 15 months, these two sections should
have given you a deeper understanding and awareness of
yourself and, in turn, the world around you. There are never
any definite certainties, but with an open mind you will find
guidance for what might be, and learn to take more control of
your own destiny.

THE CHARACTER OF THE SCORPION
· · · · · · · · · · · · · · · · ·

Highly intimate, transformative, and controlled, Scorpios are the
seducers of the zodiac calendar that are hard to resist. Whilst the
affection of a Scorpio can be addictive, their passion can quickly
feel possessive, so don't enter a serious relationship with this
intense sign lightly. If you get on the wrong side of this powerful
sign, whether it's by hurting them or someone that they fiercely
love, then prepare yourself for an almighty sting from this
Scorpion's tail; just as their love is unforgettable, so is their
scorn. Associated with the genitals, Scorpios may struggle
to separate themselves from their sexy reputation, however
private they keep their love lives.

Scorpios are perhaps the deepest of all the water signs and so
can require some extra patience and searching to get to the
core of their mysterious self. Scorpios have a negative energy
that means that most of their emotions will be kept internal,
however, they might like to express their emotions through
writing, like Scorpio poet and novelist, Sylvia Plath. This sign
doesn't like to allow itself to be vulnerable, (remember their
rather sensitive associated part of the body), so trust and
loyalty may be hard won. This Scorpion is quick to protect
themselves and their loved ones from any harm so may keep
their armour up until they decide it's safe to let someone in.

Born in the middle of autumn, Scorpio is a fixed sign that may
enjoy security and can be single-minded in their approach
towards reaching their goals. Co-ruled by Mars and Pluto, these
astrological bodies give Scorpios a controlled and competitive
attitude that will generally mean that they end up getting what
they want out of life once they set their mind to it; take the

three Scorpio Jenners, Kendall, Kris, and Caitlyn, as perfect examples of Scorpio's sexiness, controlling nature, and ability to transform.

THE SCORPION

Terrifying for most people to behold, the venom in their tail perhaps not helping, the Scorpion has a fierce reputation that some Scorpios can most certainly live up to, however, there is so much more to this creature than just their sting. Throughout a scorpion's life, it will shed its exoskeleton when it becomes too small and emerge larger and more powerful than before. Scorpios may experience a similar transformation within their lifetime, whether it's shedding their childhood as they move away to university, deciding on a change in career in their later years, or an internal transformation of some kind. Whilst the scorpion and Scorpio go through these changes they can be at their most vulnerable as their new-found selves fully form. However, once the transformation is complete both will reveal themselves stronger and more powerful than before. The scorpion is a predatory and defensive creature. Just like a Scorpio, they can go after what they want and are prone to lash out if they feel confronted. A nocturnal animal, Scorpios may also enjoy plenty of partying on nights out in their younger years; find them in the clubs shining under the ultraviolet lights like the mysteriously glowing scorpion!

PLUTO AND MARS

Renamed a dwarf planet in 2006, Pluto co-rules the sign of Scorpio with Mars. Pluto's demotion has made it no less mysterious to onlookers and its secrets are yet to be fully understood, which makes it a fitting ruler for the secretive Scorpio. Named after the Roman God of the Underworld, this planet is associated with power and depth, just like the emotionally deep and controlling sign of Scorpio. The measured power from Pluto teamed with Scorpio's other ruling planet, Mars, makes for a sign that has controlled energy with plenty of drive and fight. Named after the Greek God of War, Mars is linked with passion and can feed into a Scorpio's possessive and sensuous nature. From Mars, Scorpios can find the courage to go after what they desire, both in their personal and professional lives. Born in the eighth house in the zodiac calendar, which is associated with regeneration, the power of Pluto and the strength of Mars mean that Scorpios can hold huge potential for transformation and may choose to reinvent themselves several times over.

ELEMENTS, MODES AND POLARITIES

Each sign is made up of a unique combination of three defining groups: elements, modes and polarities. Each of these defining parts can manifest themselves in good and bad ways and none should be seen to be a positive or a negative – including the polarities! Just like a jigsaw puzzle, piecing these groups together can help illuminate why each sign has certain characteristics and help us find a balance.

ELEMENTS

Fire: Dynamic and adventurous, signs with fire in them can be extroverted. Others are naturally drawn to them because of the positive light they give off, as well as their high levels of energy and confidence.

Earth: Signs with the earth element are steady and driven with their ambitions. They make for a solid friend, parent or partner due to their grounded influence and nurturing nature.

Air: The invisible element that influences each of the other elements significantly, air signs will provide much-needed perspective to others with their fair thinking, verbal skills and key ideas.

Water: Warm in the shallows and sometimes freezing as ice, this mysterious element is essential to the growth of everything around it, through its emotional depth and empathy.

MODES

Cardinal: Pioneers of the calendar, cardinal signs jump-start each season and are the energetic go-getters.

Fixed: Marking the middle of the calendar, fixed signs firmly denote and value steadiness and reliability.

Mutable: As the seasons end, the mutable signs adapt and give themselves over gladly to the promise of change.

POLARITIES

Positive: Typically extroverted, positive signs take physical action and embrace outside stimulus in their life.

Negative: Usually introverted, negative signs value emotional development and experiencing life from the inside out.

SCORPIO IN BRIEF

The table below shows the key attributes of Scorpio.
Use it for quick reference and to understand more about this fascinating sign.

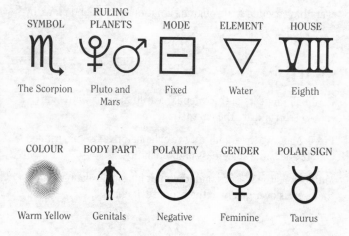

SYMBOL	RULING PLANETS	MODE	ELEMENT	HOUSE
The Scorpion	Pluto and Mars	Fixed	Water	Eighth

COLOUR	BODY PART	POLARITY	GENDER	POLAR SIGN
Warm Yellow	Genitals	Negative	Feminine	Taurus

ROMANTIC RELATIONSHIPS

· · · · · · · · · · · · · · · · ·

When it comes to Scorpio's relationships, there is no dipping your toe in with this water sign, their love is more like plunging head first from the highest diving board. The intensity of sexpot Scorpio's affection can be scary for some and less-daring signs may feel intimidated by their passion, but those that are brave enough to take the plunge will be rewarded with Scorpio's exhilarating and all-consuming love. A Scorpio might have their partners jump through some hoops to test their loyalty, but it's only to see if they are as serious about the relationship as the Scorpio is; only then will Scorpios really open up to their partners. When Scorpios fall in love it is truly, madly and deeply with their heart, body and soul.

In a long-term relationship, this fixed sign can have a steadfast approach to the one they love; there's nothing fickle about Scorpio's feelings. A committed Scorpio is loyal and protective and will always come to their partner's defence. Potential partners will be attracted to sexy Scorpio's charisma and enigmatic charm, but only the lucky ones will know Scorpio's deepest secrets and feelings as this secretive sign will only share these with a chosen few in their lifetime. Once a Scorpio lays claim to their chosen partner, their passionate love can turn into an obsessive jealousy if they're not careful.

With the influence of Pluto, Scorpios may experience some power struggles in their relationships and with their warring planet of Mars guiding them, disagreements can turn into a battlefield if emotions run high. Possessive Scorpios should try to resist controlling their partner and give them as much autonomy in the relationship as necessary, especially with individualist and free-spirited signs like Aquarius and Sagittarius. Regardless of what has set Scorpio to attack mode, if a Scorpion is arguing with their lover it is because they think they are worth fighting for. If you are an angered Scorpio or fighting with one, try to turn that intensity into passion rather than rage.

ARIES: COMPATIBILITY 2/5

If it's passion Aries desires in a relationship, a Scorpio could be the perfect sign for romance. However, this match might be too controlling and combative for long-term happiness. Both ruled by the planet Mars, these two may come into this relationship armed and ready to fight. Scorpio's controlling tendencies could be a source of many of arguments. If this fire and water duo can work out a balance of control and ease the Scorpio lover's jealousy, then these two could have one steamy relationship rather than being left hot and bothered.

TAURUS: COMPATIBILITY 5/5

Scorpio and Taurus are each other's opposites on the zodiac calendar so cosmically share a special relationship both in their differences and similarities. The element of Taurus is earth and Scorpio's water which usually will mean that both partners will provide something that the other desperately needs. Love and passion are both driving forces for these two. Scorpio has the reputation for being the sexiest of signs and Taurus the most beautiful, so a physical relationship should be strong here. Whilst this couple will no doubt enjoy each other's bodies, their tendencies towards possession and jealousy will need to be kept in check.

GEMINI: COMPATIBILITY 3/5

Passionate debates could be on the menu for a Scorpio and Gemini love affair. The water sign of Scorpio will bring emotional depth to the relationship whilst a Gemini's air influence will help breathe a fresh perspective on things. Scorpios risk suffocating Geminis with their intense emotions if turned toxic. Geminis can be flirtatious which can trigger Scorpio's jealousy, but Geminis aren't scared of a little arguing, in fact they quite like the stimulation. Being a fixed sign, Scorpios value steadiness so may find flighty Gemini too unreliable, however, this relationship has the potential to be full of spice and interest.

CANCER: COMPATIBILITY 2/5

These two water signs can easily get lost in each other's emotions. Ruled by Mars, Scorpio's passion for their Cancerian lover will be intense and a Cancerian will likely be highly attracted to a sensual Scorpio. Both the Scorpion and Crab can be stubborn and unwilling to bend to their partner's wishes if they don't match their own. Claws and stingers at the ready, disagreements could see both sides getting hurt and might end with them parting ways quickly. However, once these two decide that they want to be together, they can experience a love that is unfailing in its loyalty.

LEO: COMPATIBILITY 1/5

The love between water sign Scorpio and fiery Leo can be one of deep intimacy or dampened spirits. Here are two fixed signs that could clash in their different approaches and refuse to yield to each other's strong personalities. Shared assets, particularly money, could prove difficult for a Scorpio and Leo. Scorpio is born in the eighth house where shared possessions are important, and Leos belong in the fourth house where a love of gambling lives which could result in conflict for the couple. If respect is exercised regularly between these two lovers, theirs is a closeness well worth protecting.

VIRGO: COMPATIBILITY 5/5

Placed two apart on the zodiac calendar, the passionate and loyal bond between the Virgin and Scorpion is a special one. Orderly Virgos will value the steadiness of fixed sign Scorpio, and similarly the loyal Scorpio will appreciate the faithfulness that many Virgos are known for. With their complimentary elements of water and earth and their matching negative energies, this typically introvert couple will enjoy the nourishing effects of spending quality time with each other. Theirs is an intimate relationship but not without some passionate arguments thanks to power ruled Scorpio's influence of Pluto and Virgo's sharp tongue.

LIBRA: COMPATIBILITY 2/5

When the planets align for Scorpio and Libra, the combination of loving Venus, passionate Mars, and powerful Pluto can make for an intimate and stimulating love affair. The emotions of a water sign and mindfulness of air can be a harmonious pairing so long as a Scorpio and Libra are on the same page. Libras can seem superficial to the deep feeling Scorpio, but thankfully when this head-and-heart ruled couple fail to understand each other, Libra's charm and diplomacy can help calm any troubled waters. This love won't be without conflicts, sorry Libra, but it could be loyal and long-lasting.

SCORPIO: COMPATIBILITY 4/5

Was there ever a couple more deeply and desperately devoted to one another than Scorpio and Scorpio? The intimate connection that these two mysterious introverts can make is both in mind and body. They both can be guilty of passionate outbursts, particularly with jealousy, and their fixed attitudes can lead to arguments if they can't agree. If these two can patiently hold their breath in stormier times then this is a relationship that could sail off into the sunset together. Scorpio and Scorpio are a true power couple that, thanks to their hardy Scorpion nature, can withstand plenty.

SAGITTARIUS: COMPATIBILITY 2/5

Sagittarius and Scorpio can have a daring partnership; whether their gamble on each other pays off is another thing entirely. The adventurous Sagittarian will help expand Scorpio's horizons and appeal to their brave side, whilst Scorpio's fixed attitude can teach the flaky Sagittarian to stay motivated and see things through. The love of Scorpio can be all encompassing and the worst thing for a Sagittarian is for them to feel like their partner is at all possessive. This is definitely not a boring love, but flexibility and growth are both key for these two getting the most out of the relationship.

CAPRICORN: COMPATIBILITY 5/5

When Capricorn and Scorpio set their sights on each other, these highly dedicated signs could be in it for the long run. Placed two apart on the zodiac calendar, theirs is a devout bond that is likely to be highly compatible with matching negative energies, complementary elements, and harmonising cardinal and fixed modes. A Capricorn can offer the security that Scorpio desires and Scorpio can be the powerful influence that feeds Capricorn's ambition. Scorpio will bring the fun and Capricorn will bring the itinerary to go with it. If they can take it in turns to rule the roost, their love could go the distance.

AQUARIUS: COMPATIBILITY 1/5

Mysterious Scorpio and unique Aquarius may well find themselves attracted to one another, but the Scorpion and water sign Aquarius may need to work hard to keep their relationship off the rocks. Positive Aquarians are outgoing, and socialising in their communities is important, but this contrasts with introverted Scorpios who tend to have a small and intimate circle of friends. Their modes are both fixed which means they can be resistant to changing their contrasting outlooks. If stable Scorpio can embrace this air sign's free-spirited nature and rational Aquarius can provide the intimacy that Scorpio needs, then these two could find their happiness.

PISCES: COMPATIBILITY 4/5

Here are two water signs that will go to the ends of the Earth, or rather the depths of the oceans for one another. Pisceans dream of finding that fantasy love and the enigmatic Scorpio can be just that for them, whilst the empathetic Pisces can be the kindred spirit that secretive Scorpios can finally be vulnerable with. A Piscean's mutable nature, that flows with change can be at odds with the steadfast approach of a fixed Scorpio, but their differences mean that they have plenty to learn from each other. Emotional security and sensitivity are where these two thrive.

FAMILY AND FRIENDS

. . . .

The negative energy in Scorpios means that this sign is quite happy to spend time alone, however, even if they do not actively seek out new friendships, the bonds that this sign will make are extremely important to them. Scorpio's group of friends is likely to be small as they value quality over quantity. Each friend of a Scorpio will have been carefully selected and may have gone through rigorous tests set by their Scorpion comrade to prove their worthiness. The reason for Scorpio's caginess comes back to their fear of letting their guard down and exposing themselves to pain. Trust is an important practice for any Scorpio who wants to experience the benefits of close friendship.

As with most relationships, whether it be friends or family, finding common interests is key to forming and maintaining bonds. Secretive Scorpions could adore a good mystery, so a day out solving an escape room or a night in discussing this month's thriller book club choice could be two great ways for a Scorpio to bond with their suspense-seeking friends; Virgo's methodical analysis could make them the perfect partner for helping Scorpios get to the bottom of a crime, or an extrovert Leo friend will no doubt jump at the chance to arrange a murder mystery in a spooky house for all of their friendship group to enjoy.

Another passion of sumptuous Scorpio is food and drink, whether it be opening an expensive bottle of wine at home or enjoying the tasting menu at the latest Michelin star restaurant in town. Scorpio's negative energy could have them spending all day at home, whipping up a gluttonous feast for their family and friends to enjoy, whom likely will be quite familiar with Scorpio's culinary talents. Venus-ruled signs Libra and Taurus are friends that will happily indulge in Scorpio's love for luxury and will probably be the ones bringing over the bottles of champagne to their Scorpio host.

Scorpios can be emotionally intuitive parents; if there is something amiss with Scorpio's child, or any family member, this sign could readily pick up on it and be set on fixing whatever the problem is for their loved one. The Scorpion's love for their family is intense and their protective nature is formidable to challenge, so loved ones should rest assured that Scorpio has their back through thick and thin. The possessive and jealous side of a Scorpio could rear its unsightly head when it comes to those that this sign treasures most. Scorpio will indeed love their family like treasure and they will no doubt be the most valuable thing in this sign's life, but they should avoid treating people like possessions and trust their family to always return to them. Empowering their friends and family rather than using their own power over them will be key in maintaining happy and successful relationships for Scorpio.

MONEY AND CAREERS

. . . .

Being a certain star sign will not dictate the type of career that you have, although the characteristics that fall under each sign could help you identify the areas in which you could potentially thrive. Conversely, to succeed in the workplace, it is just as important to understand what you are good at as it is to know what you are less brilliant at so that you can see the areas in which you will need to perhaps work harder to achieve your career and financial goals.

Committed Scorpios aren't inclined to flit between jobs, unless they are still figuring out what they want to set their mind to. Scorpio's immense dedication may well see them stay in the same job or working for the same company for many years, whether they are 100% happy in it or not. A Scorpio devoted to their career should make sure that it comes from a place of passion rather than complacency. Scorpios can value security above their job satisfaction, and if they fear failure then they may decide to not try anything too daring. Channelling the influence of Mars, Scorpio should dare to dream and actively chase after their career goals with courage.

Scorpio's single-minded approach to life can mean that they lose themselves obsessively in their work, so it helps if they are passionate about their career. A sign as mysterious as Scorpio will often be attracted to the obscure or shadowy and won't shy away from darker occupations. Whether it's making an indie horror film inspired by fellow Scorpio Martin Scorsese, writing a thriller novel, or working in a funeral home, what might give other people nightmares could be the Scorpion's career calling.

MONEY AND CAREERS

Scorpios tend to be very private, especially when it comes to their bank accounts; asking a Scorpio about their salary could feel like asking them to strip down to their underwear. However, it might be clear from Scorpio's lavish spending habits as to how well they are doing financially. High earning jobs certainly will suit the shopaholic Scorpio who enjoys treating themselves to the very best of everything. Remember, this sign is about quality over quantity so whilst their shopping bags may be few, what lays inside them is likely to be of high value. The secrecy around spending and their funds may mean that they choose to keep some of their finances under wraps, even from their spouses.

Whilst you can't always choose who you work with, it can be advantageous to learn about colleagues' key characteristics through their star signs to try and work out the best ways of working with them. Hardworking Capricorns can bring structure and order to the work life of a Scorpio and make sure their passion for a project does not fizzle out before it has reached fruition. Signs with a strong influence of Mercury, like Virgo and Gemini will offer their thoughts and opinions willingly to a Scorpio seeking advice and can be important colleagues to bounce ideas off.

HEALTH AND WELLBEING

. . . .

The scorpion is known for being able to withstand almost anything, freeze this creature solid and then thaw it out and this durable wonder can still be alive! Similarly, Scorpios (minus the freezing bit) can endure serious hardship and deep emotional grievances. These folks are certainly made of hardy stock, but their water element can make them feel pain more deeply than most and make their inner power hard to channel at times. Scorpios are undoubtedly strong, but their tendency to isolate themselves in times of stress can sometimes weaken them as they close themselves off to any outside support. This controlling sign may struggle to ask for help and allow their vulnerability to be exposed, but asking for help is never a sign of weakness and should only help strengthen Scorpio.

When a stressed-out Scorpion is feeling overwhelmed, they can turn to escapism for an immediate solution to their problems; bingeing on box sets, wrapped up in a blanket, and still wearing their pyjamas may be a familiar scenario. Whilst cocooning themselves away like this, with a trashy movie, may feel initially comforting they should be careful of doing this too regularly as it could also start to have the reverse effect. Losing themselves in a good book or spending time with an Aries or Leo friend who they have not seen in a while could be a far more positive distraction. Hearing about the problems of others may give some healing perspective to Scorpio's own issues, or at the very least will strengthen their friendship ties and make both parties feel happier from having taken the time to catch up.

HEALTH AND WELLBEING

Whilst this sensitive sign may be the best of all the water signs at controlling their emotions thanks to the influence of Pluto, Scorpio's sting of aggression will usually pierce their victim with the strongest of venom. Fortunately for everyone, Scorpion's scorn is usually infrequent, but trying to avoid big bursts of aggression is still an important lesson for this sign to learn. Scorpios can have a wonderful sense of humour, so trying to channel a lighter mood that allows them to laugh at life rather than going on the attack will hopefully diffuse any internal aggression from building up. Scorpions are intense by nature and their serious side is dominant, but inviting fun into their lives and not taking things too seriously should help to balance out their moods.

With the influence of Mars and Pluto, Scorpio can have a lot of powerful energy that if left unreleased can cause emotional and physical discomfort. Teamwork isn't always a Scorpio's forte, their negative energy and fixed mode lends itself well to working alone, however, a little healthy competition can really fuel Scorpio's energy, so signing up to a running or swimming race could rid Scorpio of their restless energy and set positive goals for them. If it's a surplus of emotional energy that is building up in this water sign, then finding ways to sensitively release what is inside of them is also imperative; writing poems or a novel could be a positive outlet for this emotional sign as well as always seeking out professional therapy if necessary.

Scorpio

....

DAILY FORECASTS
for 2021

OCTOBER

. . . .

Friday 1st

Today, you're likely a force to be reckoned with. The Moon in your career sector brings your leadership skills to everyone's eyes. You can be ruthless and make any necessary adjustments needed. There are issues surfacing from your psyche, and you're prepared to deal with them head-on.

Saturday 2nd

People who are closely related to you will frown upon your boldness right now. Let them; you're working towards being authentic in all that you do. That is bound to upset someone. Venus in your sign is helping you to value yourself and build your self-esteem. Work with her.

Sunday 3rd

You'll likely find yourself wishing to spend time with friends or simply engage on social media with your wider interest groups. Mercury retrograde is still excavating your deepest self, so be prepared for something big to come up today when he contacts Jupiter. Conditioning and family issues may be the subject of revelations today.

Monday 4th

You may struggle a little today when the Moon opposes Neptune. This is a position where you contemplate your role within friendship groups. Think about how you serve others and how you sometimes sacrifice your values to keep the peace. Hold off from agreeing to anything, even if it's simply asking someone to come back tomorrow for an answer.

Tuesday 5th

Are you being observant? Stay alert to people who may try to manipulate you, as this will throw you off-track. It's OK to say no. You have Venus cheerleading for you as you stand up for yourself. This afternoon, you are more introspective and need time alone.

Wednesday 6th

A new moon occurs in your hidden sector. Both the Sun and Moon meet your ruler, Mars. Your secondary ruler, Pluto, also turns direct today. This is fantastic energy for you to access and use for setting goals regarding your inner self. Change yourself from the inside out.

Thursday 7th

Venus leaves your sign. Make her happy by demonstrating that you have learned the value of being authentic and true to yourself. The Moon drops into your sign and your emotions verify that you're ready and committed to the hard work of self-improvement.

Friday 8th

The Sun is sitting with Mars for a few days. Determination, motivation, courage and strength are yours to arm yourself with now. This may worry a lover or close relationship and cause a few niggles. Stand up and assert your right to be authentic, but do this with a compassionate heart.

Saturday 9th

Today you can be romantic or idealistic, if just for a moment. Something will make you reminisce and put a smile on your face. Mercury backs into the Sun and Mars, and you may need to shut off and listen to your inner voice of reason and encouragement. Try not to drift away too far.

Sunday 10th

Saturn turns direct. This is good news, as the teacher planet brings tough lessons and may now dish out rewards. You should be feeling outgoing and inspired. The saying 'wind beneath my wings' will ring true for you. What will you do with this energy? Anything is possible now.

Monday 11th

Stay with the momentum and get things done. Your bank balance and home require your attention. Use that empowered energy to clean, tidy and declutter things in your home that have been neglected. Make your environment lighter and less stressful. This evening you will pull back and do more serious work.

Tuesday 12th

Today you're more methodical. You haven't run out of steam; you've simply changed your tack to look at issues that have been ongoing for a while. These could be courses of study or work projects. You may need to make a lot of phone calls or emails today. Make the most of this energy to get organised.

Wednesday 13th

When the Moon meets Pluto, you have the power to bring something to closure. Maybe a project is complete, a deal has been signed or you scrap an idea that has not worked out. Venus and Saturn help you to look at what brings you joy or not. Use this to give yourself a stronger direction.

Thursday 14th

When the Moon meets Saturn in your family sector, you may need to step up and take charge. It's your turn to be firm and fair and lead by example now. No thinking outside the box today, as that will cause further problems. Everyone must play by the rules. Lead by example.

Friday 15th

You get a bonus from the Sun in your social sector. Family life and wider groups can combine to make innovative decisions. Jupiter is involved, so expect this to be big. People are expecting the deeper truth to bring them joy. Try not to disappoint them.

Saturday 16th

Take the opportunity to use the weekend for romance or art. Today's energy brings you more inspiration, but this time you can use it to connect, be spiritual and express yourself. You may have a moment of crisis, but this can be used as a trigger or a catalyst to create something grand.

Sunday 17th

Jupiter turns direct today in your family sector. More pressure is lifted and you should experience an injection of optimism. Listening to your inner voices is important, as you'll get a feel of the direction in which you are meant to go. Many planets are supporting your growth right now.

Monday 18th

Mercury also turns direct now. He hasn't finished diving around in your psyche, although he will now clear away the debris and should give you some clarity. This afternoon you're fired up to get on with mundane jobs, and catch up people you may have neglected recently. Check on your health now, too.

Tuesday 19th

The Moon sits opposite Mercury. You may get an emotional tug which causes you to start making plans. Get out your planner and make a vision board. What new things would you like to initiate? This could be huge, seeing as Jupiter and Mars are involved. You should realise that nothing is beyond your means at this stage.

Wednesday 20th

This afternoon, a full moon in your health and duties sector shows you where projects, concepts or habits have been forever changed. You may feel some regret, but there are also things to celebrate. You should look at your achievements this year. By evening, you should rest as this energy can be draining.

Thursday 21st

The Moon's monthly visit to your relationship sector meets Uranus but squares off with Saturn. This can be troublesome, as Uranus disrupts the status quo and Saturn is restrictive. Try to use this energy to brainstorm new ways of relating and bring in some excitement to your relationships.

Friday 22nd

Your rulers aren't playing nicely. There may be much to do, and you must stay in control. However, energy from Mars is in your hidden sector and you may wish to use it for your own purposes. You will need to balance both and see to your duties first.

Saturday 23rd

The Sun enters your sign, signalling the arrival of your birthday month. Happy birthday. Your mind is probably extra busy now, thinking and communicating about the deeper issues of life. Philosophical concepts may fill your head. You must listen to dream messages or wisdom from elders today.

Sunday 24th

The Moon and Venus are facing each other. Venus is ready for an adventure, but the Moon is undecided. This is a great time to interact with others and get your intellectual juices flowing.

Monday 25th

You're uplifted and should feel ready for the working week. There's no time to be dragged off-course by Neptune, so try to stay focused and optimistic. Serious discussions can stimulate your tastes for the bizarre or taboo today; you may delve deeper than before and find that you enjoy it.

Tuesday 26th

The Moon in your travel sector is always a little tricky. There's a nagging urge to expand your borders, which actually makes you do the opposite. This is more to do with taking a financial risk and your fears of instability. Take it one step at a time.

Wednesday 27th

Uncomfortable energy can make you feel manipulated or the victim of passive-aggression. The sensitive Moon sits opposite Pluto, who likes to be in control. Mercury is squaring off with the Moon, so you may have some reservations about working on your unconscious material. There's a strong chance that you fear being exposed in some way.

Thursday 28th

This morning you find your courage again and hold your head high. Venus and Jupiter, the two luck-bringers, are helping you to achieve harmony in family situations and your own self-worth. This influence may also bring financial gain. Do your job with true conviction and you will be noticed.

Friday 29th

Today you face Mercury's findings in your hidden sector. This may cause some problems with a lover or an important person. Alternatively, it could also shake things up to a point which has been long overdue. Pressure released from this area of life will leave space to breathe.

Saturday 30th

Exerting your will over another isn't a good idea, as Saturn is watching how you treat people. Mars has come to your sign, so expect to experience some fireworks. An ending and a new beginning are possible. Keep a level head if you can, as this has the potential to be an explosive time.

Sunday 31st

With the Moon in your social sector, you may wish for a peaceful time with close friends. You may be spontaneous and call up someone for a meet up. The Moon and Sun are in a good connection; use this energy to have light-hearted fun today.

NOVEMBER
....

Monday 1st

The Moon drops into your hidden sector. You may become reserved and introspective now. This is the time of the month where you find that your inner voices tend to speak to you the most. You process recent feelings and try to justify your own behaviour patterns. Some of these are no longer helpful to you.

Tuesday 2nd

You might feel that you're having a hard time, as Mercury and Pluto are squaring off. Pluto asks for permanent change and Mercury is trying to communicate this to you. This may also manifest externally as projects you have been working on. Responsibilities and adult duties are questioned now. What can you release?

Wednesday 3rd

The Moon sits with Mercury. Your head and heart are having a conversation and doing more justifying than usual. Don't make any decisions just yet. Listen to both sides and wait until you have clarity or ask for help. You may not have all the facts at the moment.

Thursday 4th

This is a promising day for opportunity, as you have a new moon in your sign. Having just passed your ruler and opposing Uranus, you may feel something is getting ready to explode in your face. This is your big chance to set intentions regarding yourself and only yourself.

Friday 5th

Venus moves into your communications sector. Here, she will mediate and research anything you wish to learn. Mercury is at the final degree of your hidden sector, so it is imperative now that you ensure you have received his message and are ready for the next steps in your self-improvement plan.

Saturday 6th

Mercury and Venus are in talks today. Do you have any questions or avenues you wish to explore? Your communication skills will be honest, direct and compassionate. Consider courses of study or work advancements and how you can set these in progress. You're ready to widen your world just a little.

Sunday 7th

A fiery Moon placement in your finance and worth sector gets you to look at what you value the most. This may be beauty, connection, hard work or money. Don't let Neptune drag you into unrealistic thinking; be honest with yourself and keep it real.

Monday 8th

This is a lovely day for being authentic and communicating your desires. Venus greets the Moon and women's wisdom is highlighted. Time spent with teachers and guides will fill your soul and inspire you to follow a strong sense of direction. You could surprise yourself and a lover with how innovative you are.

Tuesday 9th

The Moon meets Pluto in your communications sector. You have the emotional strength to deal with any changes today. Indeed, you may be making some of your own. Looking at things from a different perspective is helpful. Get creative around solving a problem and working towards a goal.

Wednesday 10th

Family time will always bring out the individual in you.
You can impress others who may underestimate just how
important your unique nature is. Mercury and Mars join
forces in your sign, and you say what you mean and mean
what you say. You're powerful today.

Thursday 11th

Big emotions are evident in your family sector. This could
cause some upset, as Uranus is connecting to this too. You
may need to shake someone out of old energy patterns and
make them wake up to the present time. They might see
you as being rebellious, but you are revolutionary.

Friday 12th

The Moon drops into your beautiful creative sector. You're able
to express yourself through art, poetry or love. This lovely energy
opens you up to connect with divine sources or simply your
higher self. Don't hold back; this is good for you.

Saturday 13th

You're on a roll and must keep up the momentum. Mercury
and Mars in your sign are both powerful allies, right now.
Use them to help you stay focused and ask for what you want.
When the Moon meets Neptune, you are dreamy; remember to
keep one foot on the ground.

Sunday 14th

You stay in the poetic zone until this afternoon, when your thoughts become more rational. You're highly motivated and desire to get on with things. Last minute weekend duties may be rushed but you should be satisfied that nothing has been neglected. Protect your energy and check your health today.

Monday 15th

Difficult energy between the Sun and Jupiter may feel like a clash of egos between yourself and a person in authority. You may fall out of favour but, as Saturn is involved, you will ultimately do the right thing. Don't take it personally, stay responsible and well behaved.

Tuesday 16th

Communications are strained today. Pluto is attached to both the Moon and the Sun. Your ego is delighted, as you're in control of an awkward conversation, but deep down your emotions are struggling with it. You may suffer a sleepless night because of this, as you're likely to dwell on it.

Wednesday 17th

This is another tricky day when you must think twice about your reactions and responses. Mars, the planet of war, is opposite Uranus, the planet of disruption. This occurs over the difficult sectors of self and others. You will feel this in your important relationships. Be mindful and pause before responding.

Thursday 18th

The best thing you can do today is to stay home and hide under the duvet. There's a lot of tension in the air, which is directly affecting your confidence to relate well. You just cannot say the right thing. It's best that you lie low until this passing moon phase is over.

Friday 19th

The full moon in your opposite sign is the reason for this trying time. What has come to light regarding your relationships? Change has happened or is imminent. There's nothing you can do now, except to accept that this is necessary.

Saturday 20th

You may feel some relief as the Moon shifts, but your mind will be busy. You must process recent events and try to emotionally detach. Step back from the drama and let your thoughts and emotions unfold naturally. This isn't a process you can rush, so let it run its course and try to accept it for what it is.

Sunday 21st

You're not getting any closer to working out how you feel right now. The Moon holds your emotions firmly in the sector of intimacy and deep enquiry. It's up to you to learn to be rational and non-judgemental, and that includes not judging yourself. Stay logical for the moment.

Monday 22nd

Today the Moon shifts into your travel sector. You desire to stay home and be nurtured. Lick your wounds and allow another to take care of you now. Stay protected in your comfort zone and let your inner child be soothed by a maternal figure who is wise and intuitive.

Tuesday 23rd

The Moon and Venus are facing each other. You must look at the roles of mother, father, inheritance and legacy. What does all this mean to you? It may mean that you have to deal with past conditioning and adjust it to adult life. Other gentle energy will help you do this.

Wednesday 24th

Mercury is at the final degree of your sign, and asks that you mull over recent hurts before he moves. The Sun is already in your finance and value sector, which indicates that you may get a new lease of life for your home or a boost in finances. Be bold as you move forward.

Thursday 25th

A strong Moon in your career sector gets you back on your feet to deal with adulting and responsibility. Mars in your sign is connecting well to Venus, which can signify a reconciliation or simply getting what you desire. Step up and ask for something, a pay rise even. Just don't be greedy.

Friday 26th

The fiery Moon opposes Jupiter today. You may find that a person in authority will challenge you. Speak your truth, for Jupiter can represent the law and changing fortunes. Deeper truths are waiting to be discovered, so set your sights on them. Move forward on the path you are destined for.

Saturday 27th

Your heart and head may not be in sync today. Connect with your wider social groups who may be able to help you get some clarity. Question everything today and make an informed decision if one is required. Try to keep your emotions out of anything important and be open and ready to receive good advice.

Sunday 28th

If you listen well, you may be surprised at what you hear. This will concern your friendships and relationship, and will be beneficial in the long run. You will need to be grounded today as, when the Moon opposes Neptune, you will be in danger of misrepresentation.

Monday 29th

Mercury is in the heat of the Sun and asks that you listen to everything today. Dreams, messages, gossip and guidance will all help you at a later date. The Moon is back in your hidden sector, where you form opinions about recent events and people you have encountered.

Tuesday 30th

Saturn is the biggest influence on you today. This firm but
fair teacher is asking you to show how responsible you are.
Your finances and value system will be questioned. Look
around you and see what, in your home, is keeping you small.
Can you let it go now?

DECEMBER
. . . .

Wednesday 1st

Neptune turns direct. You will now see issues regarding your
creative sector in a clear light. The time has come to use your
muse and put your romantic and artistic endeavours to work.
The Moon drops into your sign and you become empowered.
Follow your passions.

Thursday 2nd

Although the Moon is opposite Uranus, you can use this energy
to create positive sparks in your relationships. You're supported
by Neptune and Venus. Put your heart and soul into a long-term
project. Remember to abide by the rules of etiquette and you
won't go wrong.

Friday 3rd

The Moon meets your ruler today in your sign. Your personal
energy and drive will have an emotional attachment. It's possible
that you clash with a leader or elder in the family. Be respectful
but don't keep yourself small. There is more to let go of now.
You're moving on.

Saturday 4th

Today there's a new moon in your finance and values sector.
You may have a goal or intention that you think is wildly
unattainable. Don't discard it. Have a talk with your inner self
and, if this is truly worth your while, then reach for it.

Sunday 5th

You are outgoing and upbeat today. An air of optimism surrounds you and others are attracted to it. Checking your finances and starting a savings pot is a good idea now, as Jupiter is involved here and he expands all he touches. This afternoon there may be visits or messages to attend to.

Monday 6th

There's useful energy for getting things done, and remember that communication with lovers, such as sharing your dreams, will prove fruitful. Both of your rulers are working together to make you assertive, productive and goal orientated. Try catching up on work or projects you have neglected.

Tuesday 7th

The Moon meets Pluto today and also connects to Mars. Your personal energy is ongoing. You will see something come to completion now, or you may even scrap a project that has become a burden. Your family of origin may have a get-together or some news for you today.

Wednesday 8th

Stern words within your family are possible now. You may see a battle of wills where someone has to back down to keep the peace. Tension will only be released if there's respect and healthy boundaries. Mars connecting to Jupiter may blow tempers out of proportion. Deal with the fall-out when you're calmer.

Thursday 9th

Sometimes, it's better to keep the peace than to speak your truth. Today is one of those days. You will not get anywhere by being your usual, intense self. If there's drama around you, walk away and don't rise to it. Stay in a neutral place for now.

Friday 10th

Today is much quieter. The Moon has moved into your creative sector. If you need to say your piece, do it with art, poetry or music. This is a much safer way of using the unpredictable energy coming from Uranus today. You have an impulse to create and love.

Saturday 11th

You may get lost in a daydream or in your art. The muse is strong in you right now and you're urged to begin a long term or difficult project. Venus meets Pluto, making this into beautiful, transforming energy. Neptune lets your emotions drift without a care. Take this chance to allow yourself to be emotionally and creatively free.

Sunday 12th

Venus and Pluto are discussing endings, beginnings and new cycles of life. They are in your communications sector, so prepare for serious discussions about recycling something old. The Moon in your health and duties sector is eager to please and work through a checklist. Keep it real and attainable.

Monday 13th

Two planets shift signs. Mercury enters your communications sector. Expect a lot of business lunches and brainstorming now. Mars storms into your finances and value sector. Put your energy into making money and creating a home to be proud of. You can be ruthless with decluttering.

Tuesday 14th

Sweet talking over a candle-lit dinner with a lover is on the menu today. Earth energy from the Moon and Mercury provides you with an opportunity to make solid plans together. You will stay grounded and be practical. Enjoy the delights of a tasty meal or get sensual.

Wednesday 15th

The Moon meets Uranus and you may feel the Earth move today. The combination of emotions and instability can go two different ways today. Stay mindful, as you may experience volatile feelings bubbling up. This energy can also manifest as positive electrical charges and fireworks. Maybe it's time to celebrate the season early?

Thursday 16th

Today is also filled with good energy for lovers or self-care. Neptune connects and shows you what is possible in a relationship when you look through the eyes of the other. Venus and Pluto ask you to look at making or recreating something beautiful. Work at finding the hidden gold.

Friday 17th

You have a mini-crisis today, which may involve money.
The festive season can be expensive and today you may
feel that your money is being leaked out in all directions.
Check on finances you share with another or on other
investments. Maybe you can pull some back in now.

Saturday 18th

Venus turns retrograde tonight. She will turn away from
Pluto and retrace her steps in your communications sector
for several weeks. Recycling projects will be on hold now.
You may see the return of an old lover or have a new
interest in a project you have previously discarded.

Sunday 19th

A full moon in your intimacy sector will illuminate where your
mind is busy with enquiry. You may have been researching a
deep and intense subject and can now grasp the concept of it.
This Moon may also help to settle an indecision or two. Late
morning, the Moon shifts and you crave security.

Monday 20th

Your head and emotions do battle today. It's possible that your
to-do list is so long that you cannot face it. This is harmless and
is only you reacting to feeling a little overwhelmed. If you need
to have a meltdown, punch some pillows. Then sleep on them.

Tuesday 21st

The winter solstice ushers the Sun into your communications
sector. Give yourself time to pause in this busy period. Reflect
on the year gone by and contemplate how much has changed.
The longest night will bring you dreams and messages, so listen
carefully. Trust your intuition now.

Wednesday 22nd

The Moon is now in your courageous career sector, but this is no time to stand out from the crowd. Join in the festive fun but remember to play by the rules. Family needs are important now, too. You may have to decline an invitation to the office party as you have duties to attend to.

Thursday 23rd

Today is an auspicious time of stillness from the planets. Jupiter is at the final degree of your family sector. This is a clear statement about where you should be now. Share the joy of the season with your nearest and dearest. Let your unique light shine.

Friday 24th

Social invitations from your wider groups come in, but you're obliged to consider where you are needed most. Think carefully as the more disruptive planets are connecting and tension is building. Be of service today and do your best to co-operate. Tempers may flare in the evening.

Saturday 25th

The celebrations are here, and the planetary connections suggest a level of high activity and chatter. Sacrifices may need to be made of your time. Venus retrograde bumps into Pluto today. Watch out for subtle manipulation tactics or passive-aggression. Be prepared to help out and encourage others to do the same so that all the work doesn't fall on the same person or people.

Sunday 26th

You have managed to survive a day that some people find testing. Venus and Pluto both connect well to the Moon today and you should feel emotionally stable. Take some time this evening to unwind, detach from others and process your thoughts alone. Listen to your dreams tonight.

Monday 27th

Today is reasonably quiet. Your energy returns with some help from your ruler. It is possible that you act as a go-between or you are asked for wise judgement on a matter. You are good at seeing both sides of an issue and others come to you for that.

Tuesday 28th

You need time alone or with a very select group. The Moon is in your hidden sector but squares off with planets that can cause you unrest. Your mind will be full from the last few days and you may judge yourself too harshly. Try to find the value somehow.

Wednesday 29th

The Moon is in your sign. Of course, the monthly opposition to Uranus can be unsettling but you must work it to your advantage. Have a lively, fun time with a partner. Jupiter enters your creative sector for the next twelve months. This is highly beneficial; lucky you.

Thursday 30th

Mercury and Pluto meet up today in your communications sector. You may talk yourself into taking on a huge new project or ending one now. This is a day where you can dream big and put your own self first above everything else. Self-care is essential now; remember that Venus taught you that.

Friday 31st

The end of the year sees the Moon meet the point of past karma and also Mars. This occurs in your finance and values sector. You know what did not work this year, now forget it and march on. Enjoy the celebrations with your head held high.

Scorpio

....

DAILY FORECASTS
for 2022

JANUARY

· · · · · · · · · · · · · · · · ·

Saturday 1st

Happy New Year and welcome to 2022. Your year begins with a sense of agitation or tiredness. There is a shift happening within relationships, but you don't seem to have the energy to deal with it today. Take a day off from over-thinking and worrying about things that haven't happened yet. You don't need to be productive today.

Sunday 2nd

Discussions with family may highlight radical new ideas and more involvement this year. A new moon allows you to set intentions regarding things you might like to learn. A long-term study project can be planned carefully if you look at all the required steps involved.

Monday 3rd

A ghost from the past could come back to haunt you or display manipulation tactics. You must try not to get sucked into a victim mentality and deal with this by putting your own interests first. Emotional cords may need to be cut, or old wounds need to be healed.

Tuesday 4th

Your heart and head are in talks and you could be fighting with your conscience now. This may affect your current relationships negatively. By evening you may have more sense of what the right action is to take. Personal boundaries are essential if you wish to keep things respectful.

Wednesday 5th

Think about your core values today and they may keep you on track. An open heart and altruistic nature may be desirable, but you're driven to seek the truth, however much it hurts. Stay true to yourself and remember your own worth. This is not something you should compromise on.

Thursday 6th

Emotions may be overwhelming today, and you could become entangled in idealistic thinking. Romance and creativity may benefit from this influence. Restless energy suggests that you should be cathartic and use your talents to express yourself with poetry or art. You may get dream messages and prefer to work with those.

Friday 7th

Today can feel quite dreamy and surreal. You may be more inclined to follow a whim and check in with your inner compass. Where is your true north pointing? Are you on track? Stay away from people who may try using power games to get you on side.

Saturday 8th

Physical exercise would be a good activity for you today. This is something which could get rid of excess energy and help you to think more clearly. Processing your thoughts whilst pushing your body could blow away some cobwebs and bring you clarification on recent issues. Aim to detox certain parts of your life this year.

Sunday 9th

Tricky issues from the past, maybe ex-lovers, could come to a head today. This won't be easy to deal with unless you maintain a mature and respectful manner. You could become more assertive and wish to engage with conflict if only to get it sorted once and for all.

Monday 10th

Your dreams and ambitions could be feeling unattainable now, so you must ensure that you're putting your energy into the right things. Too many projects on the go could be confusing and drain your energy. Partner time can help you to look at the bigger picture this evening.

Tuesday 11th

It's possible that you're argumentative today. Maybe you can't seem to say the right thing to anyone. It might be a good idea to lie low until this energy passes, or you could risk an upset within your important relationships. Think about your core values and put effort into aligning with them.

Wednesday 12th

You could have triggers from your past relationships via messages or gossip. However, you're in a better frame of mind to deal with them and don't let them spoil your day. You may be more forgiving now and accept that past events taught you valuable lessons.

Thursday 13th

Mercury turns retrograde tomorrow, so do all the necessary preparations today. Back up all devices and double-check travel plans. An emotional pull towards your future options can take up mental energy and distract you from current problems. Don't go down a rabbit hole unless you're prepared for a few revelations.

Friday 14th

Your family life may be more affected by Mercury's first retrograde of the year. You must take care not to start a revolution or go off on a tangent now as this will be a detour you will have to backtrack. Use this time to review projects you've planned with a group.

Saturday 15th

A restless night can leave you feeling drained and uncertain today. Take some downtime and nurture yourself. It might be a day to do something you love such as cooking favourite foods or watching TV shows that thrill you. Planning trips can also be satisfying.

Sunday 16th

Conversations can reveal a secret or two today. It could be that harsh words are spoken, or unexpected events take place which are disturbing. This might feel as if you're being dragged from your happy place and you may feel over-sensitive and resentful of the intrusion. Exercise your right to say no.

Monday 17th

Drifting back to your safety zone may be premature today as you could feel more defensive. Triggers and old wounds may be raked up again and the full moon might highlight where you feel vulnerable. Take care of your own needs and retreat from conflict if you need to.

Tuesday 18th

Uranus turns direct today and you may feel some pressure being released within your love relationships. You might begin to have more idea of where you wish to grow this year. It could be that your individual talents need to be exposed and earn you some money. Do some research on this.

Wednesday 19th

You may just have to go with the flow today. Pushing your own agenda won't get you anywhere. Family members could frustrate you and one-to-one relationships can be of little help. Try not to voice an opinion now as it could be unwelcome or ignored.

Thursday 20th

Put your attention into your value system today. You may benefit in the workplace if you're seen to be going the extra mile with something that you're passionate about. Your friends and social groups could be a good way to unwind this evening, but don't make issues bigger than they are.

Friday 21st

You could surprise yourself by thinking outside the box today and getting rid of an annoyance. Friends and social groups can be supportive and give you a healthy and honourable way of dealing with troublesome issues. Communication is the key now, so be extremely clear with your meaning and listen carefully to others.

Saturday 22nd

If you feel slightly adrift or off-centre, take control of things you can transform or end permanently. Once again, this can be done with precise communication. This may take a lot of physical or grounded energy but will be beneficial in the long run. Redress your energy balance by resting this evening.

Sunday 23rd

Today you must take a break from trying to do everything yourself. There may be an urgent issue to deal with concerning finances, your home or your values. However, take care to listen to advice from family members first. Weigh it all up before acting.

Monday 24th

Mars, your ruler, enters your communication zone and you could find that you have more energy to assert yourself with study, research or long-term projects. Do the right thing by making sure you're aware of all the steps needed to make something that others will pay attention to. Advice may come from an elder or boss.

Tuesday 25th

The Moon drops into your sign and you could feel more like using your detective-like skills to get to the bottom of an issue. Remember not to take anything personally now. Your drive and emotions are working together to get results, but Mercury could still trip you up.

Wednesday 26th

There may be trouble brewing with someone from the past. You need to be crystal clear when discussing this or toxic will remain with you for a longer period. If you daydream and romanticise this, you could get into trouble. Remember your personal boundaries and those of others.

Thursday 27th

You have a great chance today to throw something old into the cosmic waste bin and dispose of it forever. Don't mess this up. You need truth or answers, but you may have to accept that closure won't be coming your way. Search your soul for the reasons you need this.

Friday 28th

Matters of the family can be your driving force today. You could be blazing a trail and others may notice how outwardly seeking you are. Truth, justice and fairness are important to you and you may be prepared to put your own visions aside to attain these.

Saturday 29th

You might be surprised today as troublesome issues from recent weeks seem to evaporate or get solved with little conflict. It could be that you've taken back control and are no longer letting someone emotionally manipulate you. Put extra effort into building a solid future for yourself and dream big.

Sunday 30th

Today you may relax and come back to a sense that you are worthy of great things. Relationships could surprise you and take a positive new turn. You can return to your inner compass and concentrate on your dreams and visions now. Get back on track and align yourself and your values.

Monday 31st

Your heart may be in the right place today, but be warned that Mercury could rock the boat. It's likely that you speak openly and share too much which can leave you more vulnerable than you'd like. Home, family and your roots can be a place to return to for comfort.

FEBRUARY

. . . .

Tuesday 1st

A new moon can get you to look at your family and community. If there's something you would like to contribute to and make a difference, now is your chance to sign up. This may be the outlet you need to get rid of excess energy and to turn your attention outward.

Wednesday 2nd

Romance and creativity are highlighted now. You might be thinking about how to add more beauty and passion to your life. Artistic ventures may be pleasing and give you a boost. Love can be the inspiration you require to get something of value off the ground and kick-started.

Thursday 3rd

Your emotions can be high today and you could be swept away to a fantasy island or distant planet. You might surprise yourself with the strength of your feelings. Try to look for an anchor as grounding these feelings will be more beneficial than letting them drift and flow.

Friday 4th

Your inner compass is right before you. Grab hold of it and align with what you believe to be true and just. Mercury turns direct and you might be going back over old ground for a third time. You would be wise to listen to the advice of an elder in your family today.

Saturday 5th

Pay attention to your health as you might find that your energy levels are waning. You may need a rest day being nurtured by your family. There's no point trying to climb a mountain today or starting a long-term project. Simply do the necessary and limit your duties.

Sunday 6th

If you try to do too much today you could find that you're getting nowhere fast. Your missions will have to wait until the energy is better. This evening you can enjoy partner time and allow yourself a little luxury. Just be careful not to project your frustrations onto your loved one.

Monday 7th

As your mood and energy lifts, you could notice that you're more productive. This can make you feel good and in turn, lift your spirits even higher. Be prepared for an exciting night as your partner may also be pleased by your better mood.

Tuesday 8th

You could be extra stubborn today and wish to get your own way too much. You must look at everyone's needs and come to an agreement or compromise. Use your inner compass to guide you in making responsible and mature decisions. Dreams and wishes seem more possible to attain now.

Wednesday 9th

Today you could have a pull towards your future goals. There may be something that you need to assimilate into your life now. This could concern, relationships, values, money and quality. You could be accepting a slower and more pleasurable pace of life in the coming months.

Thursday 10th

Looking deeply into your own psyche never scares you and continues to fill you with fascination. However, you may feel overwhelmed or lost today. Subconscious material could surface, and you may be unsure what to do with it. Think about it for a while. You may need a spiritual advisor or group for support.

Friday 11th

Going with the flow would help you more than fighting against it today. Be flexible and open to change or new ideas. If you stay alert you may have a new mission or interest which could take up a lot of mental energy. Decluttering your inbox could pinpoint something you've neglected.

Saturday 12th

The celestial lovers, Mars and Venus are getting close now. Their union can mark the end of one cycle and beginning of another regarding love, passion, tradition and hard work. You may be open to merging with the collective or prefer to snuggle down with a loved one this evening.

Sunday 13th

Think about your security needs today. What makes you feel safe may also expose the softer and more vulnerable sides of you. This could be something which you wish to keep hidden, but with Mars and Venus meeting, you may need to reconsider how you relate and share with others.

Monday 14th

Be careful what you say today. There is potentially a window for you to speak your mind, but you will need to take extra caution as this may backfire on you. Don't say anything you can't retract or back up. Work issues may come to a head.

Tuesday 15th

You might get frustrated today and need to let off steam somehow. Stick to the rules and be respectful and responsible as you may not be the only person with stress about this. Try to merge your compassion with your drive in communications as this will be beneficial in the long run.

Wednesday 16th

Mars and Venus meet under a full moon. You could be stepping up your game and showcasing what you can do in the workplace. This can mean that you use your emotional and physical drives to get things done to great effect. Social groups can be supportive this evening.

Thursday 17th

Today you could be emotionally drained and need to get rid of excess energy in a safe place. Your love relationship can be the right place for you to do this and with Venus and Mars still conjoined you may have an intimate, surprising and joyful time with the one you love.

Friday 18th

Social and shared interest groups may be a source of encouragement and can entice you to continue doing well in communicating your needs. This might feel like you're going against your inner compass' dreams and wishes but is actually a part of it. Embrace the change and flow with it.

Saturday 19th

Process recent events in your own time today. It could be that you have an inner conflict which needs to be reconciled. Your head and heart may have a little talk and you will need to ignore the voice of your personal critic and find your cheerleader instead.

Sunday 20th

Get all your duties done today and leave time to contemplate your next move on the road to your personal growth. This might not be easy today as you could have too much going on in your head. Find peace by doing something for you alone. Private time is essential.

Monday 21st

You may have an idea of something which needs to be removed from your life to make more space for new things to come in. The Moon drops into your sign and your emotions could be more intense than usual. This is the time when you're more likely to overthink.

Tuesday 22nd

Disturbances deep within you may bubble up and you could be at risk of projecting these onto your lover. However, if you can avoid this you could be more aligned with your partner than you first thought. Maybe they share your dreams and visions and can show you empathy today.

Wednesday 23rd

Get rid of excess emotional baggage now by throwing it to the universe and looking ahead not backwards. You may be more inclined to seek joy and optimism in others or to find the beauty in your home environment. Remember that you are worthy of being part of the wider world.

Thursday 24th

Search within yourself for the answers you seek. It might be that you believe you need to get out and see the world to find out who you are, but introspection and deep study of yourself will serve you better. Self-discipline may be needed for you to put a few things straight.

Friday 25th

You could struggle today as you reach for your inner compass and guide, but it's nowhere in sight. This is a sign that there are other more pressing things you need to do today. Settle into some hard work and get productive as this will always make you feel good.

Saturday 26th

A pleasant surprise or revelation may occur in a close relationship. It may be a day trip or short travel experience where you can satisfy your urge to get away. You can also benefit from merging your creativity with your romance and coming up with an innovative way to entertain a lover.

Sunday 27th

Feel into the great energy around today. You could be in a position where deep emotions and desires combine to get you back on track with your core values. A path may open up before you and you should take a leap of faith and follow it.

Monday 28th

Try not to be too radical today. You may be wishing to push boundaries within your family or test new ground that you're unprepared for. Also, be careful with your words. You could reveal too much too soon. Alternatively, you could say what's on your mind with an open heart.

MARCH

· · · · · · · · · · · · · · · ·

Tuesday 1st

Family values may need to be assessed today and this could produce challenges in several directions. Pause and reflect on what has gone before and how things need to proceed. You would do best to listen to advice or take a mature and responsible approach. Get creative and innovative.

Wednesday 2nd

A new moon in your romance zone might be the green light you need to set intentions and goals about changing relationships for the better. Be sure to listen to the opinion of your significant other. Art projects are also favoured under this influence, so think outside the box.

Thursday 3rd

You may be dreaming about future possibilities and what you need to discard in order to grow this year. If you notice a big shift happening, let it play out. Your desires and drive to obtain them are working in sync. All you need to do is get a game plan ready.

Friday 4th

Pay attention to your health today. You might not notice when you are beginning to feel burnt out and continue to work hard. Give yourself a break. This may seem counter-productive but will help you see things clearly and in an organised manner. Methodical decluttering will help.

Saturday 5th

Watch out for ego trips today. You could be exaggerating feelings of romance and making grand gestures. Make sure you can back them up. However, if you're genuine, this can be a day filled with blessings, insights and revelations. Always remember to play by the rules and follow guidelines.

Sunday 6th

Venus and Mars move into your family zone together. This can be useful if you need to use more compassion and energy in group projects which are for good causes or humanitarian purposes. You may also feel like a new phase is starting where you must be more open to working with others.

Monday 7th

Agitation or excitement can kick start your day and keep you moving forward. Partners may notice how empowered you are. The pleasures and luxuries of life are more attractive at this time, but you mustn't ignore your duties or you'll be frowned upon. Work first, play later.

Tuesday 8th

You could have a glimpse of your future goals and how to manifest them. Conversations may not flow so easily as people will be more stubborn today. Your mental energy might be doing overtime now, and you could be digging deep into your own psyche or researching mysterious topics of interest.

Wednesday 9th

There's a lot of emphasis on your family of origin right now. It could be that your roots and childhood are subjects that you need to revisit for answers. Look at triggers and see if you can get to the bottom of why you react the way you do.

Thursday 10th

You could become more curious now as Mercury enters your romance and creative zone. This might be the best time to find your muse and express yourself from the depth of your heart. Deep and intense issues can fascinate you but can also take you away from your true north.

Friday 11th

Home is where you feel safe and nurtured. It's also where you obtain food for your soul and feel part of the bigger picture. You may be reminiscing about travelling or planning a new trip to a beloved part of the world. Friends from abroad could be more nurturing than family now.

Saturday 12th

Allow yourself some luxury and comfort today. Partner time may give you the chance to cook your favourite foods, entertain with good company, music and a favourite movie. Indulge yourself and give your senses a treat. Romance is high on the agenda, so cosy down with your loved one.

Sunday 13th

Your true north is glowing today, and you may feel a calling to create, make love or express yourself openly. You could also be swept away with nostalgia and attempt to recreate that feeling. Stay in control and keep one foot on the ground as you drift away to a fantasy island.

Monday 14th

Today you could come back down to earth with a bump. Work or daily duties distract you from your happy place and you may feel resentful. This will pass, so stick to the job in hand and try not to be too grumpy. Your leadership skills may be required.

Tuesday 15th

Challenges may come if you resist being told what to do. Standing up for yourself is good unless you're doing it out of spite or belligerence. You might come across as a stroppy child or set in your ways. Self-righteousness doesn't suit you, so lie low until your mood lifts.

Wednesday 16th

As your emotional energy shifts, so does your approach to daily life. Your social circles may be the place where you let off steam and get rid of a bad mood. Introspection with like-minded friends can help to put things into perspective. Detox your mind and free up some space.

Thursday 17th

You may not feel much like following a dream today. It could be that you feel the need to do a practical activity or apply collective knowledge to certain themes. Leave your creative projects for today and set your mind to being part of a group which offers unconditional love and service.

Friday 18th

Today's full moon may highlight where you've been overloaded with unnecessary baggage. It may be time for a declutter of your inbox, friends list or daily duties. Learn to delegate and not take it all upon yourself. Quiet time to process this will be available this evening.

Saturday 19th

Your thoughts can flow easily today if you allow yourself the time and space. You may discover something which makes you uneasy, but with careful thinking, you can balance this and justify it to yourself. Don't beat yourself up about historic events which are still playing on your mind.

Sunday 20th

The spring equinox arrives and emphasises the need for balance in your most private mind. You could have a lot of things you wish to initiate, but know that other things which no longer serve you will need to go. It's okay to grieve your loss, but don't dwell on it.

Monday 21st

The Moon is in your sign and you could be bouncing off the walls today with impatience and a deep desire to start new things. You must get things down on paper today before you lose your train of thought and can't retrieve it. Try not to project your restlessness.

Tuesday 22nd

Make the most of the deeply intense energy today to be
your best self. Research, study or simply following a trail of
unusual enquiry can suffice. Transform something old or
come to terms with a karmic issue. Keep busy this evening by
organising and beautifying your home environment.

Wednesday 23rd

Listen carefully to your dream messages. Look out for symbols
which can be meaningful only to you. This is a time when
your intuition can be more astute. Gut instincts need to be
followed. You could be awash or overwhelmed with creativity
now, so get messy, speak your truth and romance your lover.

Thursday 24th

You could be feeling the exact opposite of yesterday, but
don't worry, this is just a reality check and there are probably
mundane things needing your attention. You may have
overspent and could now be worrying about finances.
This is a temporary challenge, so ride it out.

Friday 25th

Your duties can help to pass the time, but you need to be seen
to be trying. Put your back into your work now and stir up
some interest in your dedication. Communication is the main
theme today. You must be professional at all times and others
will treat you likewise.

Saturday 26th

There's a time to dream and a time to work. Today you might achieve the perfect balance and stay in control of all your obligations. Conversations can be supportive and encouraging. Keep listening out for subtle hints and messages. There could be an especially important one arriving today.

Sunday 27th

A new mission may have been revealed to you which might take up a lot of time and effort. However, if you take care of your health this can also be invigorating. You could have more inspiration now and find that you're keen to include this in your daily routine.

Monday 28th

Watch for mood swings today as the Moon touches planets in your family zone. You may be open to adding your voice to a good cause but could also be doing it for selfish reasons. You must be sure that whatever you choose to participate in, you do it for the greater good.

Tuesday 29th

A dreamy mood may take you away to an imaginary world where you can go with your own flow and make music, poetry, beauty and love. This is lovely energy, but you must be sure to remain realistic. You could also be taken for granted under this energy, so take care.

Wednesday 30th

The energy today is more excessive and can be dangerous if you choose to use substances to switch off. Everything is exaggerated and surreal. You may feel that this is bliss and wish to stay longer. However, you could be looking at this through rose-tinted glasses.

Thursday 31st

Your mood changes now and you realise that you might have neglected your duties. This might mean that you're busier than usual. As always, keep a check on your health and don't go overboard in an effort to make up for lost time. Keep a low fire burning and work steadily.

APRIL
. . . .

Friday 1st

A new moon allows you to set goals and intentions regarding
new plans. These could include your health and fitness or your
mundane duties. This would be a good time to minimise your
obligations so that you don't become overworked and stressed.
Delegate jobs and schedule time for yourself.

Saturday 2nd

Start putting things in place which can raise your self-worth
and maintain healthy boundaries. You may need to have a
tricky conversation with someone who has been pushing your
limits and expecting too much from you. Give yourself a well-
earned treat this evening.

Sunday 3rd

Listen to any dream messages and symbols you might have.
You may see a signpost which can point you in the right
direction to serving others unconditionally whilst not being
taken for granted. Expect a few surprises or revelations within
your love relationship today. Your emotional side may be
itching to do something unusual.

Monday 4th

You could feel out of sorts today. This may come from having
to make changes which involve your family obligations. Try
not to feel guilty about letting people down just because you
have said no to them. This is a protection tactic you need to
exercise more in the future.

Tuesday 5th

A low mood continues to knock you back. You might experience conflict with an elder or have to be assertive with someone. This might go against your nature but is necessary. Venus enters your romance zone, so prepare to be lifted up and to learn what holds meaning and value for you.

Wednesday 6th

Let your mind wander today. If you end up down a mysterious rabbit hole with intense feelings, let them rise and see what you can learn from them. You may even find that you laugh at yourself for taking something too seriously. Be light-hearted and sociable. Today you can play.

Thursday 7th

Family matters might be on your mind and you may need to be mature and lay down the law. This can be tiring and cause you distress, so give yourself time this evening to do something you love. You might need to retreat and take some time to recharge.

Friday 8th

Your intuition could be higher than usual today. If this is the case, you should make use of this with your creative projects. The energy suggests that some of your best work can be done today and you may surprise yourself. Put your personal drive into what matters for the moment.

Saturday 9th

Keep doing what your inner compass tells you is right. It's likely that you feel more aligned and can get creative or romantic easily. Try to avoid getting involved with others unless they make you feel nurtured and inspired. Make the most of the blessings that are available to you now.

Sunday 10th

Your emotions may turn outwards now, and self-expression can be your outlet. However, this can also make you feel under attack and need to defend or assert yourself. This may not be the case and you could just be sensitive to perceived limitations on your personal time and energy.

Monday 11th

Mercury enters your relationship zone. Communication between yourself and important others can become pleasurable and grounding. This can move your partnerships up a level if you can converse respectfully and avoid conflict. There may be some stubbornness involved, but you can work this out by keeping the lines of communication open.

Tuesday 12th

You could expect your own way today and this can cause tension in the workplace or with family members. You may wish to retreat into your creative zone and continue making your dreams and visions a reality. Social groups can be chatty and help to ground you.

Wednesday 13th

Your self-worth may take a nose-dive today, but this will pass. Try not to get involved with people who might take you for granted. Be there for others but don't commit to something which feels wrong. Stay grounded and do something practical to occupy your mind with other things.

Thursday 14th

Today might present some challenges. There may be something urgent to do regarding your family of origin and this may raise further issues. Your physical energy could be drained and might leave you feeling at a loss regarding your creativity. Settle in for a quiet evening alone to process your thoughts.

Friday 15th

There are now four planets in your romantic and creative zone. Although this is good news if you wish to be productive, it could also mean that you get overwhelmed and tired easily. It's important to find practical activities to do when this happens as you might feel lost at sea.

Saturday 16th

Today's full moon can expose parts of your psyche which are out of balance. Pay special attention to what comes up now as there is scope for you to deal with these issues. Relating, equality and how you merge or disconnect from life can be the themes to heal now.

Sunday 17th

The Moon in your sign can bring intensity, but as a Scorpio, you are used to this. It can mean that you put more effort into your romance and can be more probing and enquiring. You may be more direct under this influence and can say what you feel without filters.

Monday 18th

An emotional roller coaster of a day can bring up volatile emotions which are projected onto a partner. You could be delving into areas which aren't for you and will need to recognise boundaries. As a result of disappointment, you may turn to your art or poetry to pour out your emotions.

Tuesday 19th

Today you feel the need to uncover the truth. You might think something is being hidden from you. Finances and your value system appear to be what drives you today. You might find money leaking out to old subscriptions you no longer use. Be honest and fair.

Wednesday 20th

The Sun enters your relationship zone and heats up your partnerships. You may become more optimistic about your shared future and plan future pleasures. However, your emotional side could be racing ahead of itself and you might come unstuck. Slow down and plan properly or you could mess this up.

Thursday 21st

Take today one step at a time. There may be a lot of messaging, research, study or visits to be done. You must start at the beginning and follow the natural route even if it takes longer than you'd like. Your ruler, Mars, helps you to maintain focus and direction.

Friday 22nd

This is a lovely day and could set the tone for the weekend. If you remember to communicate your feelings and not miss anything, you could be heading towards a more than amicable time with a lover. There is excitement, desire, conversation and dreams all waiting in the air to be experienced.

Saturday 23rd

Listen to a partner and let them have their say today. You may be having in-depth discussions on what makes you both tick and you'll need to pay attention. It's possible that the two of you are making plans for the future and can factor in your family unit too.

Sunday 24th

A stubborn edge might prevent you from enjoying the remainder of the weekend. It could be that family obligations get in the way of your partner time. You must do what is right and respectful and prioritise your duties before leaving time for others. There may be harsh words spoken.

Monday 25th

Family issues might play on your mind and leave you restless and agitated. Personal space may be needed and can provide you with an outlet for your anguish. Try to put something down on paper or find a spiritual practice to centre yourself. Yoga or meditation might help.

Tuesday 26th

You could have a clear idea of what makes you tick and put extra energy into getting more of that. This can be exciting and radical. A new path might open for you to explore, but you shouldn't act on impulse. This may be a detour that isn't good for you.

Wednesday 27th

Be incredibly careful today as you're in danger of drifting off into your own little world. If you persist in following a dream or indulging yourself today, keep it safe and make sure you are aligned with your inner compass.

Thursday 28th

Today you might come back to your earthly activities and decide that what you really need is a clear-out. This may be a case of making physical space and letting go of material goods which you no longer need. It may also be that you have a clear and direct talk with a partner.

Friday 29th

Pluto turns retrograde today. This will herald a time where your status can shift or evolve. You may notice that a new cycle starts or that you lose something which has been holding you back. If you tend to accumulate more than you need, expect unnecessary things to disappear.

Saturday 30th

A new moon and solar eclipse open a window of wild card energy in your relationships. Be on your guard now and don't take anything for granted. Your creative and romantic zone is blessed by good fortune today, but in eclipse season, this may be short-lived.

MAY
· · · · · · · · · · · · · · · · ·

Sunday 1st
You could be compelled to do something unusual today. A visit
to somewhere new to you could be a good idea. Alternatively,
you may wish to stay indoors and wine and dine a loved one
with exotic food. There could be words of love that you are
impatiently waiting to express now.

Monday 2nd
A dreamy and optimistic mood can take over your morning. Be
mindful that this doesn't interfere with your duties. You could
be investigating deep issues within yourself and looking for
your inner guide to light the way. Ensure that you know the
way back as this could be an emotional roller coaster.

Tuesday 3rd
Your mind and energy could be scattered in several directions
today. Try not to push against the flow as this will drain you.
This is a good time to look carefully at all your options and
projects. Which ones are taking up too much of your energy or
not achieving much?

Wednesday 4th
Challenges persist in making you question the worth of your
creative projects. You may also find that a love relationship
is not satisfying you today. This is a passing phase and simply
means that you need to do practical activity and think less. Try
an innovative approach to love.

Thursday 5th

Your own needs come into focus today. Are you getting them met? There is unstable energy surrounding these issues and you could be forced to consider whether a relationship is giving you what you need. Protect your boundaries and recognise what feels like home and you may have a startling revelation.

Friday 6th

Discussions with yourself could expose gaps in your knowledge of deep psychological issues. Be kind to yourself and forgive yourself for what you didn't know. Emotions may be on the edge and you could be chasing a lost dream or settling into a new one. Let your energy dictate this.

Saturday 7th

You might get the feeling that something needs urgent attention in your creative and romantic life. Positive thinking can keep you afloat if you're unsure what this is. It can make you a little vulnerable. Speak up for yourself this afternoon and get things off your chest.

Sunday 8th

Fiery energy can cause you to behave irrationally today. You may feel like the compassionate warrior and have a busy day doing things for others. However, this can have an adverse effect on your one-to-one relationships as you may be too stubborn to accept that you need to slow down.

Monday 9th

There is an edge to your personality which you come pretty close to today. This can be your way of being defensive or outspoken but could mean that you clash with authority figures. Be aware of any boundaries which you mustn't cross, or risk being frowned upon by those above you.

Tuesday 10th

Mercury turns retrograde today. This can be a tricky few weeks where you will need to go back over recent thoughts and research into your own psychological workings. Back up devices, double-check travel plans and refrain from committing to anything important until you've had time to review what is being offered.

Wednesday 11th

Do something physical today. Jupiter bounces into your health and duties zone and as he expands everything he touches; it might be a good idea to join a gym. It's especially important that you don't take on too much and ignore your health over the coming year.

Thursday 12th

You might be trying to balance your inner turmoil or reconciling past events to yourself. Thoughts may not bring you comfort today as they could be muddled and confusing. It's best not to take anything for granted right now. Balance the small things instead or use this time for rest.

Friday 13th

A small conflict could arise today, but this might be your conscience speaking. You could be worried about finding time for yourself and also neglecting your mundane duties. Remember that your mental health is important, and this should come first. Others can wait and if they can't, you must delegate your chores.

Saturday 14th

Intense feelings could be making you irritable today. You may be grieving a loss from long ago. Raking up the past won't help you, so put your energy into your romantic relationships and let your partner lead the dance. It will do you good to let go of control.

Sunday 15th

Try not to project your frustrations onto a partner. Instead, let them listen and give constructive advice. Take a good look at where your energy is being spent and where you can let something go. A future dream calls, but you may need to be patient before activating this.

Monday 16th

A full moon and lunar eclipse in your sign can be extremely intense and probing. It can feel like you're under interrogation. Alternatively, it may throw light onto unexpected opportunities. This could give you the fuel you need to follow a dream or plan with passion and optimism.

Tuesday 17th

A simple day of getting things done can please you. Check in with your body and make plans for healthy meals and fresh air. Money matters are favoured, and you might get inspired to enhance your finances in some way. Think big and set your sights as high as you can.

Wednesday 18th

Your ruler, Mars, meets Neptune, your inner compass. This is a particularly auspicious day and can be pivotal in deciding your future plans. As a Scorpio, you need to be passionate about your goals in order to chase them. Today you can put everything you've got into taking the first steps to attain them.

Thursday 19th

Shifts are occurring and you feel these in your bones. You would do best to do practical activities to ensure that your plans are grounded and have the best compost in which to grow. This might mean decluttering your environment and making space in your schedule.

Friday 20th

Be incredibly careful today. If Mercury retrograde trips you up it's likely to be in a big way. Keep a tight control on your money and commitments. Family issues may need to be more fluid or discussed more openly. Again, these could be made unnecessarily larger or exaggerated. Keep it simple.

Saturday 21st

Today you must listen for any messages or dream symbols that come your way. Mercury is receiving downloads regarding your deep psyche and your thought processes. You could find that a course of study is presented to you which would be beneficial. Think it over but don't commit just yet.

Sunday 22nd

You might have a day of doing lots of jobs for your family members. You may feel popular and therefore will do these unconditionally. Make time for love and romance this evening, but be careful not to share too much about any thoughts you have now as Mercury is still playing tricks.

Monday 23rd

There could be an urgent issue within your romance or creative pursuits. This may take up a lot of energy and could leave you feeling muddled or in a stalemate situation. You may be tempted to act out of character and jump straight into something, but you would be better off waiting.

Tuesday 24th

Hold still and try not to do anything rash today as this could backfire on you. Your inner compass is in sight but asks that you wait around for a while and enjoy the views. By evening you might be incredibly impatient for something to happen and could do something stupid.

Wednesday 25th

Your emotions might be huge today. You may also have an appetite for exercise and going the extra mile for others. Take it easy as you may not recognise your own limitations. Be kind and respectful to yourself and others.

Thursday 26th

Tread carefully today and take any well-meaning advice on board. You could benefit from following the guidance of an elder or boss who has your best interest at heart. Family members can also be supportive and encouraging if you need to delegate some of your mundane chores.

Friday 27th

Make plans for a cosy weekend with a lover or special friend. Perhaps you haven't had enough time to treat each other lately and wish to put that right now. Think of what makes you both tick and plan for good food, entertainment or maybe a day out to a special place.

Saturday 28th

Today can be filled with surprises and warm your heart. It will do you good to have some downtime, just don't overthink everything and spoil it. Venus has entered your relationship zone, so expect to be loved up and laden with the good things in life for a few weeks.

Sunday 29th

Try to be flexible and open-minded today. You might have some resistance or blockages to your plans and will need to find a workable solution. Passion or anger could be hugely exaggerated today, so make sure that you say what you mean or retreat and say nothing at all.

Monday 30th

A new moon allows you to set goals and intentions regarding study, especially in the darker more mysterious subjects such as psychology or astrology. This might be the course you've been waiting for to understand your own workings better. Sign up as this would be great for you.

Tuesday 31st

You could struggle with a challenge today. There may be problems within the family which need your attention, but your sensitive side kicks in and makes things difficult. Keep your emotions out of it and exercise your common sense and maturity. Responsibility and respect are needed to resolve this particular problem.

JUNE
. . . .

Wednesday 1st
Conflicting feelings can make you feel vulnerable and exposed.
You could be trying to put down roots in a new place but feel
agitated about your ties to everyday mundane life. A partner
may be encouraging and support your need for security. You
can be over-sensitive and seek solace in travel plans.

Thursday 2nd
Don't be too rash today. You may be impulsive and decide on
booking a holiday which could feed your soul. However, you
must think this through thoroughly as you may not have seen
a few loopholes. Satisfy your senses with good food experiences
with a loved one.

Friday 3rd
Mercury turns direct in your relationship zone. You might find
yourself going back over issues for a third time, but with more
insight. Allow yourself to dream but stay grounded. There may
be changes or difficult conversations which feel threatening.
Stand your ground and find your voice this evening.

Saturday 4th
You have more physical energy today and might be inspired to
explore new places. This can give you the inspiration you need
to evolve. There could be many things interesting you, but you
should try not to take on more than you can handle. Saturn
retrogrades today and will teach you more about boundaries.

Sunday 5th

A stubborn attitude won't get you anywhere. It may be that you're wanting your own way and could sulk if this doesn't happen. Expect to come under scrutiny this evening as you rub up against authority figures who challenge your childish behaviour. Play by the rules this evening.

Monday 6th

Be methodical and practical today. You may need to sift through your duties and pay attention to detail. A more humble or apologetic approach to others might help, but can also build resentment. Tread carefully and look inside yourself for answers as to what triggered your poor behaviour.

Tuesday 7th

Physical exercise or sensual pleasures may help to alleviate any frustrations you might have. Your restless energy needs to be appeased and you can do this by allowing a partner to take the lead and provide good food and entertainment. Check your health as it could be a little shaky now.

Wednesday 8th

Concentrate on the job in hand and you could have a satisfying day. Being productive can help you forget about trivial worries. You may be communicating, researching or scrapping old projects which no longer serve you. Be a channel for your friends if they need your advice and opinions on something.

Thursday 9th

You possibly feel like having time alone to get a few things straight in your mind. However, the outside world calls you and there are duties and obligations to be met. It may be a challenge to face these today, but if you make a schedule, there'll be time for everything.

Friday 10th

Get the bulk of your chores done during the day because this evening you could be invited for fun and games. If things are not adding up leave them alone for now and plan for some intrigue. The intense Moon in your sign may see you playing around with exciting concepts.

Saturday 11th

Prepare for some surprises in your love life. Expect the unexpected and you could find that your senses are tantalised or that a partner goes out of their way to offer you a pleasurable weekend. You might sense that this is occurring and not understand why you feel this anticipation.

Sunday 12th

Be incredibly careful that you don't project your unwanted baggage onto a partner today. It's possible that you have an underlying restlessness which can become volatile if not tamed. This is a karmic time and you might need to stop a past issue from letting you enjoy the present.

Monday 13th

You could be more goal-driven today and this bodes well for your work environment. You may be adept at research or getting to the bottom of long-standing problems and this will raise your self-esteem. A happy and assertive approach to work can get you through the day without a care.

Tuesday 14th

Today there's a full moon which can highlight any financial issues. It can also show if where you've been setting your sights has paid off. You might need to adjust your value system slightly and review what brings quality to your life. Wider study can be enjoyable and beneficial.

Wednesday 15th

Play around with new thoughts and concepts today. There could be a huge blockage in your thinking which needs to be overcome. You might have to go back to the start and look at it in a different way. However unfavourable this seems; it may be the only way to success.

Thursday 16th

Applying practical knowledge and finding the right allies can help you make a breakthrough today. This may be more down to earth than you realise. Stop looking too deeply for a moment and take hard facts as your guide. Overthinking and too much analysing won't help, but being grounded will.

Friday 17th

Your family roots and home environment can be a source of joy today. You may be called upon to be of service to your family unit, but this isn't a problem. In fact, it's more of a joy to do today because you're more open-minded and willing to be a team player.

Saturday 18th

Don't be tempted to fall back into stubbornness and wilfulness. This could spoil anything you've developed with your family and can cause conflict you can do without. If this is about your self-worth, think twice as it may be a trigger which activates childhood conditioning.

Sunday 19th

There's better energy today and you may wish to switch off from recent troubles and find your inner compass. Music, poetry and romance may be on the menu for the day. A sensual time is waiting for you, so grab the opportunity and enjoy a good time with a lover or your inner world.

Monday 20th

Look deeply into your own psyche as there may be something which once caught your attention but was forgotten. This could be a final decision about study which has an upcoming deadline. As your inner compass becomes clearer, hold on to it and check that you're aligned with your core values.

Tuesday 21st

The summer solstice arrives with the longest day. This can energise you and fill you with optimism for the months to come. You might notice that shifts are happening naturally, and you are filled with possibilities and new options to do what feeds your soul. Enjoy this happy time.

Wednesday 22nd

You could have an emotional attachment to your mundane duties today. Your mind may be racing ahead making plans, but your body could react in a way which makes you slow down and appreciate what you already have. Sort out what is necessary and what can be overwhelming.

Thursday 23rd

Time with a partner could continue to be satisfying. You may be planning trips for the future or indulging in exotic experiences such as travel documentaries, good food and higher knowledge. A vested interest in doing more personal growth work around study can help raise your self-worth.

Friday 24th

Today can go in two different directions. There is volatile energy around which can be troublesome or exciting. If you feel restless, get out and do something different. Think outside the box and find an activity that you can enjoy with a partner. The earth might shake for both of you.

Saturday 25th

Plan for future goals now as your heartstrings might be pulled to do something more earthy and sensuous. If this is in line with your core values, it will serve you well to listen to what your heart is saying. Your inner compass approves and puts things in place for you to achieve this.

Sunday 26th

A lazy day of contemplating and thinking about the things you share with a lover or business partner could be a way of settling decisions. You can be inspired and motivated to make more plans, but as always, you could be taking on more than you can manage.

Monday 27th

Give yourself a good talking to today. Find out what it is that you want to know about yourself, your relationships and the deeper mysteries of life. Family matters might be troublesome and divert your energy, but you can deal with these respectfully and with a mature attitude.

Tuesday 28th

Neptune turns retrograde today. As your inner compass, you may find this period slightly confusing. However, it serves to get you to look at the bigger picture and to dissolve anything which is in your way. It can be disconcerting, but as a Scorpio, you will understand the value of this more than most.

Wednesday 29th

Today's new moon can allow you to set goals and intentions regarding what makes you feel safe, nurtured and looked after. Travel opportunities may come, and you must grab them as these can give your soul the nourishment it requires to feel part of the wider world. This Moon comes with many blessings.

Thursday 30th

Anticipation fills you and you need an outlet for this. Use this time to consider where you may have been thinking too small. A different perspective can let you know in no uncertain terms what needs to be discarded in order for you to grow.

JULY
. . . .

Friday 1st
This is a good day for standing up for yourself and showcasing what you can do in the workplace. Grand gestures and the willingness to go the extra mile will be noticed. You can truly shine in an authoritative position. Make the most of it and stand out from the crowd.

Saturday 2nd
You might encounter some challenges or blockages today. Use this time to review where you've been and where you're going next. You may just need a quiet day to gather your thoughts and make a game plan. If clarity evades you, leave it for another time and simply enjoy a day off.

Sunday 3rd
Organising your schedule or tidying up your contacts lists may be the best activity for you today. This can help you to get a better picture of what is cluttering up your life. Friends and social groups may require your attention for a good cause or a group project.

Monday 4th
There could be some urgency around a mundane job today. Check your to-do list and see if anything is outstanding. Groups could offer invitations for summer fun and travel. Weigh these up before committing to anything. Their idea of exploring may not match yours.

Tuesday 5th

Your ruler, Mars, shifts into your relationship zone. This can be a time of extra passion or heated arguments, so be mindful of this. Try voicing what you need to feel witnessed, protected and nurtured as this can ensure that your relationships fulfil you. Be concise and honest as vagueness will only confuse.

Wednesday 6th

It's possible that you need time alone to process your thoughts. You may have opened up too much and feel vulnerable now. If recent discussions have impacted your daily duties or your stress levels, turn within and recognise your triggers.

Thursday 7th

You could be on a trail today and digging up things from the past which have affected your current state of mind. If you can reconcile this, forgive yourself and love your inner child. You may find that family members aren't willing to go as deep as you if you approach them for answers.

Friday 8th

Your emotional needs could cause some turbulence in your relationship today. Know that this is a temporary phase which will pass as quickly as it arrived. Stay calm and try not to project any issues onto a loved one. Deep and intense self-discovery is easier this evening.

Saturday 9th

Volatile energy can bring you to your edge. This is familiar territory to you, and you should realise by now that working with this makes you grow. There may be some uncertainty or an urge to rebel, but what you should be doing is getting rid of old karma and lightening your load.

Sunday 10th

Your dreams may give you messages or indications about what is holding you back. Allow them to guide your actions today. Think big and aim your sights high and you might see an improvement in your self-worth. Agitation serves as a catalyst for change and fulfils your safety needs.

Monday 11th

Indecision weighs on you today. This could involve finances or self-worth. Perhaps you've overspent and regret it. However, you have enough fiery energy to deal with this and can come to a solution which makes you happy and optimistic for future endeavours. Don't keep yourself small today. Show up and be counted.

Tuesday 12th

Slow and steady wins the race today. You could be having many conversations which challenge your need for speed and depth. You may have to be satisfied with using a different tactic and being more physical or practical. If this irritates you, indulge in some sensual pleasures to relax.

Wednesday 13th

A full moon can show you the top of a mountain you've recently climbed. However, you may see another peak beckoning. This doesn't phase you because you enjoy a challenge. Travel opportunities seem thwarted, so you may like to bring things closer to home and keep researching exciting opportunities.

Thursday 14th

You could be too set in your ways to accept another viewpoint today. Learn to be flexible and look at successes by others. Family matters may be tiresome and cause some tension you could do without, but they can also make you feel good if you step up and offer your services.

Friday 15th

Being stubborn will hinder your progress in all that you do today. You may feel some agitation and threaten to go your own way or do something radical. Think twice now as this will reflect poorly on you. Stick to the rules and be respectful to others involved in group projects.

Saturday 16th

A change of heart lets you see where you aren't helping yourself. Look out for symbols and signposts which can show you what your soul needs. If you wish to explore other cultures and philosophies, you must first understand what makes you feel at home.

Sunday 17th

Think about what your core values are today. Travel opportunities may be incorporated into your long-term plans, but you must be realistic. You could be following a false trail or romanticising the wrong things. Partners can help to ground you and keep things real. Be open to having your mind changed.

Monday 18th

Your emotions could be off the scale today. Your artistic gifts may receive a muse or a revelation. Your inner compass tells you to strip away idealistic thinking and see through illusions. Try not to give too much of yourself away in an effort to feel loved and appreciated.

Tuesday 19th

There could be a last-minute deal you can clinch today. Travel, education and home life are the themes. Stay alert for a bargain holiday or experience. Your intuition is high now. You could be bouncing around at work and others can be attracted to your optimistic and joyful outlook.

Wednesday 20th

Slow down before you burn out. You could be so busy making changes or ending old plans that you're not paying attention to your health. There must be something you do for yourself that serves you alone. Wind down and relax this evening. Enjoy good food and your partner's company.

Thursday 21st

Don't beat about the bush today. If you have something to say, just say it. It can be laced with emotions and desire which is your natural default, but today it will benefit you more. Your partner may appreciate the extra time and attention, but be sure to keep it on equal terms.

Friday 22nd

There could be something stirring deep inside you and screaming to get out today. You may be yearning for action or unusual activity. This might rouse your inner rebel and could upset family members. You may be too stubborn to negotiate and do your own thing regardless.

Saturday 23rd

Be careful today. You may be playing a role which leads others down a dark and tricky path. Make sure that you've left a trail to help you get home again. Pushing your own agenda might give you some problems. To stay positive, stay open to suggestions from others more experienced.

Sunday 24th

You could have a choice to make today. This might involve doing your own deep personal work or jumping around for others doing mundane chores. Whichever you choose will be satisfying as both make you feel good. You may not finish what you start, but you will have a fun day.

Monday 25th

Money can be an issue today. You may be indulging in things which aren't long-lasting and will barely enhance your life. Make sure that you get quality for your money. If you make a mistake or indulge in frivolous ornaments you could regret it. Look at your basic needs instead.

Tuesday 26th

That urge to spend is still there, but you may have a better idea of what will mean more to you. Your soul's desires may be things such as food and travel experiences. You may find a home away from home if you look hard enough. A partner might disagree.

Wednesday 27th

You may be inclined to appease a partner by showing them how much they mean to you. If you consider them part of your family group, they may then realise how your need for nourishment includes their love. Shared dreams can be revisited to enforce your relationship goals.

Thursday 28th

A new moon helps you to think about what you want to achieve regarding your work and career. How would you like to stand out from the crowd? What special gifts can you offer? Jupiter turns retrograde and asks that you look at your perceived limitations and get a healthier routine.

Friday 29th

This is a challenging day where nothing you say will make the slightest difference. You might feel like giving up before you even start. However, this phase will pass, so take some downtime and lie low for a while. Don't project irritations from work onto your love life.

Saturday 30th

Be careful what you say today. You could be tempted to voice an opinion which doesn't go down too well. It's important that you remain respectful towards authority figures who have more experience than you. Be willing to accept advice and constructive criticism. Time out with your social groups can help you unwind.

Sunday 31st

You may still be incensed by recent events and need an outlet for your anger. The best thing to do today would be to go for a walk in nature, do some vigorous exercise or something completely off the wall. Think outside the box for unusual activities to enjoy.

AUGUST

Monday 1st

The energy is unstable today and you may notice that your relationships feel the brunt of it. Try to allow this to propel you into a future goal which you're passionate about. Hard work and dedication may be beginning to pay off for you. This could be a new cycle starting.

Tuesday 2nd

Take time today to process whatever has recently transpired. Look at your needs and wants and push the boat out. Financial matters may be improving, and this could surprise you. Don't blow this by indulging in futile dreams and possessions. Balance quality and quantity and make yourself feel good.

Wednesday 3rd

Partnerships may be giving you what you need right now. What you want you can get by negotiations and compromise. However, you might need more time to be alone and switch off in order to process this fully. Remain respectful if you need to explain this to your partner.

Thursday 4th

Introspection could be a theme for you over the next few weeks. You could be sorting, filtering and decluttering areas of life which can weigh you down. Friendship groups can be a burden too. As the Moon drops into your sign, your feelings may become more intense but productive.

Friday 5th

Try not to be too set in your ways today as this could lead to you undoing some of the good you've done lately. It's time to look at what can be thrown away or let go with love. This may be distressing and cause some friction which you could project onto your loved ones.

Saturday 6th

Look at things through a different lens now. Are you seeing clearly? It could be that you're still under an illusion of how things should be. Put yourself first and review what your personal needs are. This evening you may realise you've set your sights too high.

Sunday 7th

Slow down today. You could be going too fast and expecting miracles to happen overnight. Exercise more patience and look at your limitations. Keep it simple and basic as you may come up against blockages which cause you to fall at the first hurdle. Check your anger with family members.

Monday 8th

You could have a better idea of what isn't working for you now. Think about your core values and if you're aligned with your inner compass. It may be a case of going back to the beginning of the path and retracing your steps. This can help you see where you've gone astray.

Tuesday 9th

If you're feeling vulnerable today, it might be that your expectations of yourself were too high. Do something practical or make lists and schedules for yourself. If your workload is too much, you must slim it down or risk being overwhelmed and scrapping your plans altogether.

Wednesday 10th

Irritation or anxiety can keep you awake. However, this can
be useful energy for you to manage what needs doing as you
prefer not to quit or fail. Take a moment to recognise triggers
from childhood such as not being good enough. The mature
you is ready to grow even more.

Thursday 11th

Your family might demand your time today, so ensure that you
are free from other duties before agreeing. Work can cause
problems and you may take this out on a partner. Venus enters
this area now and can help you be a force to be reckoned with,
but compassionate too.

Friday 12th

A full moon highlights family issues or group ventures you've
been involved in. This may not be a reason to celebrate as
other influences suggest that this is fraught with tension. Your
shadow side may appear, and people may feel your wrath today.
Be kind and respectful or back off.

Saturday 13th

Your heart and head aren't in sync today. You may be speaking
your mind and causing problems. Alternatively, you could be
emotionally invested in something which isn't going too well.
If you're not being heard, retreat and let the dust settle.

Sunday 14th

A fuzzy head can be made clearer if you use your artistic
talents to get things down on paper. You have a chance today
to wine and dine a loved one and create special time between
you. Your inner compass lets you realign and come back to
your centre of calm and stability.

Monday 15th

You might start the working week ready to face anything. It's possible that you can break through limitations and reach a level of satisfaction for yourself and those in charge. Conversations may be interesting, and you could be negotiating financial situations with a professional attitude.

Tuesday 16th

An outgoing mood can be fuelled by success today. All eyes are on you now and whatever you do seems to have a lucky touch. Friends and social groups can be supportive and fun to be around, however, you may find that something has ended permanently, and this distresses you.

Wednesday 17th

Partner time is highlighted today, but you may come to blows over opposing opinions. Your self-expression can come across as uncaring and selfish. This might result in a mini tantrum and will not look good. Try to remember what brings you both together and stick to doing what you both love.

Thursday 18th

Take extra care today as tempers may be hot and cause disagreements. You may feel an urgent or impulsive urge to do something without thinking it through. This can result in you looking foolish and you might need to back up your actions with words. Choose them wisely.

Friday 19th

A different perspective may help you come to terms with recent problems. This might be a clash of egos or a feeling of hurt and disappointment with a loved one. Don't take it personally. Look within and try to find out why you were triggered in the first place. Let go of old wounds.

Saturday 20th

You may have a desire to make up or break up today. Think about this carefully. You might not come to a decision easily, but you could spend time looking at your deepest parts and why you react the way you do. A compassionate and flexible mind will help.

Sunday 21st

Today may be overwhelming for you and as much as you try, you just can't get your point across. It would be best to retreat into your own world and forget about things. Work on yourself and your reactions. This irritation may be telling you what needs to heal and grow.

Monday 22nd

You have a chance to shine today and show people what you're made of. You can be more sensitive and find the right words to express your feelings. Use this opportunity to put a few things right. You might have to be humble and forget your personal grievances.

Tuesday 23rd

Your sensitive side comes forward now and you could be more sympathetic towards those you may have hurt. This can make you feel like doing something unusual, but can also lead you onto a new journey where your shadow is asking to be witnessed and healed. Be open to constructive criticism.

Wednesday 24th

Uranus turns retrograde today. This unstable planet serves to shake things up if we're feeling stuck or complacent. Your relationships will feel the force of this. Meanwhile, you can look at your vulnerabilities and ask yourself why you hide them instead of facing them. Study can give you some insight.

Thursday 25th

Your motivation and inspiration combine to make you work hard and get noticed today. Make sure that you double-check your schedule and that nothing is outstanding. You could have a deadline approaching soon. Be kind to yourself and work only as hard as you need to.

Friday 26th

Plan something special for yourself over the weekend. Your mind has been taken up with big issues recently and you need a treat. Meditation or a spiritual retreat may be just what you need to get back in balance. However, this may not go down too well with family and lovers.

Saturday 27th

A new moon lets you look at what you do for others and how that's returned. It may be that this is something you have to balance. Set goals around introspection and decluttering your life. Friends and interest groups may be something that needs slimming down. Think carefully before making any irreversible decisions.

Sunday 28th

It may be useful to look at your financial obligations today. This may be another avenue which needs balancing. If you've been contributing to something, make sure that it's still valid. There could be subscriptions which no longer meet your needs and can be cancelled.

Monday 29th

Listen to your inner voice today. Try to separate your critic from your cheerleader. Mercury is in your most private part and is digging up the gold that you hide away. There may be something which you've kept hidden for fear of not being good enough. It might be time to reveal this.

Tuesday 30th

If you need time alone to process a few thoughts and concepts, respectfully retreat from your other duties. This might feel awkward but will ultimately benefit you. Others may have to wait for your service until you're in a better frame of mind. Personal time is what keeps you healthy.

Wednesday 31st

Elders in the family may be more helpful to you today. They could be the ones who give you the wisdom and support you need. You might notice something which needs to go once and for all. This may be a toxic attachment to something which no longer serves your best interests.

SEPTEMBER

· · · · · · · · · · · · · · · · · ·

Thursday 1st

A karmic issue may surface to be reviewed. Don't be drawn back into the negative feelings this produces. You've evolved since then and this could be a final test. You may also be considering resurrecting past skills or realise that you've become too comfortable with an unhelpful situation.

Friday 2nd

Hold onto your dreams and visions today. There's a lot of work to be done before they can be implemented so now is the time to make sure that they still hold value for you. Tweak it if you need to or bring an end to something which isn't working for you.

Saturday 3rd

Your imagination may have been doing overtime and you give yourself a pep talk. Your inner cheerleader supports your ability to resolve any deep issues. This can take a lot of mental energy so remember to switch off or direct your focus elsewhere to avoid burnout.

Sunday 4th

You might need to exert your influence with family members today. You can do this with the utmost compassion even if others are being awkward. Present the bigger picture in a way they can understand and put your own agenda to one side. Healthy boundaries need to be established or improved.

Monday 5th

Difficult conversations can cause you some stress and make you wonder why you bother trying to be the peacemaker. Be an open channel and listen to everyone's point of view. Fairness and honesty are the best forms of communication and today they can be the key to moving mountains.

Tuesday 6th

Hard work and dedication to your tasks can show others that you mean business. You could be causing a dust storm with the speed and efficiency with which you work. Don't let it settle before you've completed what you need to do today. Let something go with love and respect.

Wednesday 7th

Group work can be effective if all members are on the same page. However, you might have to push for more effort. Deadlines may be looming. Use all your mental powers to gather the troops and brainstorm new ideas. You might still be ruminating on this alone by bedtime.

Thursday 8th

Today can be challenging and you might feel as if you're up against a brick wall. Genius thinking is needed, and family or social groups might provide the answers. Don't give up until you've exhausted all possibilities. Stick to the rules and maintain good boundaries with respect and responsibility. A mature attitude helps.

Friday 9th

Today you are more inclined to drift away from your problems and put your focus on art or romance. Idealistic thinking can be good for these projects, but you could be neglecting your other duties. Friends and wider groups may be antagonistic now as you wish to create beauty and harmony.

Saturday 10th

A full moon in your creative zone can showcase what you've been working on. You can be extra romantic now and celebrate achievements with love and compassion for all. Mercury turns retrograde and you might find that you revisit private thoughts and review how you respond to triggers.

Sunday 11th

Take a day off and unwind in your favourite way. The energy suggests that you desire to get up and go, but your body isn't responding. You could be overly emotional or need to rest. You might think that life is unfair to you today.

Monday 12th

You may not be able to settle and focus on anything today. Your thoughts can be consumed by your own issues and you may be responding in unhealthy ways. Stop pushing into corners that don't concern you and settle for playing by the rules just to avoid extra stress.

Tuesday 13th

It might be hard to start something new today. Alternatively, you may also have difficulty letting something go. It's okay to grieve a minor loss, but don't dwell on it. Space has been made for new growth and development. Plan to indulge yourself with tasty treats or partner time this evening.

Wednesday 14th

Friends and lovers can provide you with an easy-going day. The future calls out to you and you may be contemplating what the next step is for you. Innovative ideas may come to light this evening but will need time before they are ready to seed and manifest.

Thursday 15th

You may be making changes today which align with your true north. However, these must be considered thoroughly. You may be glamoured by something attractive which is not as good as it appears. Hold fire until you know more. Research more deeply and read around a topic that is interesting to you.

Friday 16th

Once again, you could be overwhelmed or unwell. Friends and social groups may not be giving you what you need today, so make time for yourself. You could find that material from your psyche comes up for review. Do what you can to heal this with love and kindness.

Saturday 17th

Financial matters could become troublesome today. It's possible that you're behind schedule or need to rethink money you share with another. An emotional attachment to this needs to be released before you can think and act appropriately. You could feel as if your dreams will come to nothing now.

Sunday 18th

Travel and higher education may be the themes for today. It could be that your yearning to fill your soul with experiences which nurture you appear unattainable. Be careful, as you could easily fall into depression and self-doubt. This phase will pass, so ride it out by resting and lying low.

Monday 19th

Your mood might lift today, but only if you put your mind to practical tasks. This can take your mind off your security issues and help you to think clearly. Financial matters may not be as bad as you think but could probably do with a clean-up.

Tuesday 20th

If you've been kept awake by your worries, you may also have found a solution to them. Friends and social groups can offer suggestions, but ultimately, the decision is down to you. Your vulnerability might be exposed, but this is the first step to asking for any help you might need.

Wednesday 21st

Take it slowly today. Mercury could cause a few problems at work and you could resort to conditioned habits and responses which are unhelpful. You may need to delegate some duties, so you aren't overloaded. Keep it fair and balanced because your health might suffer if you take on too much.

Thursday 22nd

You have more energy today, but be sure to direct it the right way. Your opinion is needed, but your current mood may cause you to speak out and cause some tension. A rebellious attitude towards authority won't help and could add to your problems. Filter your thoughts before speaking.

· · · · · · · · · · · · · · · · · ·

Friday 23rd

Keep quiet today. Listen to what your inner voice advises.
Ignore the critic and pay attention to the voice that is cheering
you on. It may be time to show parts of yourself which are
valuable, but you keep hidden for fear of rejection. There is
more emphasis on support groups now.

Saturday 24th

Try not to overthink today. Practical activity such as
decluttering your space or organising your finances can be
a good distraction. You may have to open up and seek advice
from friends. Innovative thinking or an unusual activity with a
partner might blow away some cobwebs.

Sunday 25th

A new moon can be the green light you need to reconcile
contrasting feelings you hold deep inside. You might resolve
to do more inner personal work now. It's important that you
do what makes you feel noticed and loved today as this will lift
your spirits and clear the air.

Monday 26th

If you know what is holding you back, do something about
it today. This might be something as simple as needing to
exercise more, try a healthy diet or removing unwanted
connections from your life. You might be slimming down
your responsibilities and giving yourself more free time to
enjoy your own plans.

Tuesday 27th

Don't struggle to control something which has come to an inevitable end. Conversations can be tricky today but may clear the decks for something fresh and new to begin. You can grieve this loss and honour the place it once had in your life, but let it go for your own good.

Wednesday 28th

The Moon enters your sign and your mood lifts. This could mean that you power through the day but pay little attention to family needs or authority figures. Personal boundaries need to be recognised and respected. Prioritise your chores and be there for the people you love.

Thursday 29th

You could be raising a revolution today, but you will be on your own. The rebel inside just wants their own way and you could clash with elders or bosses. Try connecting to your inner compass and ask yourself if this is really what you want from life. It probably isn't.

Friday 30th

Today you have an opportunity to gather your resources and make them work for you. Think about the minimum you need to do to get by and how much time and effort this requires. Set your target and review this with your finances in mind. Don't go over the top.

OCTOBER
. . . .

Saturday 1st

You might take things too personally today and get very down. Be sure to correspond your feelings with the utmost honesty and respect for your family unit. You might need to put your dreams and visions on hold today and go along with the crowd's agenda.

Sunday 2nd

Mercury turns direct, but you could be in a stalemate situation with your inner compass. You might need a few more weeks before you can think clearly or learn about the next steps to take. Practical activities can help to take your mind off other worries, but don't overdo it.

Monday 3rd

Today could see a shift in your finances. This might mean that you speak to the right people who can help you move forward to success. This will also benefit your relationship and raise your self-esteem. You may have a revelation which sets the tone of your next summit to climb.

Tuesday 4th

Issues within the family could be smoothed over now, but only if you learn to say no to excess duties. This is important for your physical and mental health. Look at it as a way of looking after your own interests and keeping your stress levels down.

Wednesday 5th

Challenges can be minor and overcome today with a little help and wisdom from an elder in the family or a leader in your social groups. Your spirits can lift if you're prepared to listen and not resort to radical or temperamental behaviour. Direct your energy into seeking answers from your psyche.

Thursday 6th

Romance and creativity are highlighted for today. You might be switching off and withdrawing into your fantasy world where you can explore the depths of your art and love. You may feel like merging or connecting with others on an ethereal level. Spiritual groups can support your need for belonging.

Friday 7th

Today it's important that you recognise any issues involving communication or study. You might be reaching out or picking up a course where you left off. If you've experienced a mind fog, expect that to be lifted as your discernment kicks in and you sort the good from the bad.

Saturday 8th

You're almost at the end of an old habit or project which is no longer serving you. Get creative and complete this before picking up anything new. You may be guided by your romantic nature to look for another Holy Grail, but think twice. Taking on another big quest could be futile.

Sunday 9th

Pluto turns direct and relieves some of the pressure you've been experiencing around changes and endings. A full moon highlights your long list of goals and aspirations and which ones have borne fruit. This can teach you not to overload yourself with duties which may impact your health.

Monday 10th

You may feel driven and wish to make some headway in your personal projects now. However, you must give yourself some time to pause and reflect on what has worked for you and what hasn't. Be confident in your abilities to do well. You don't have to prove anything to anyone.

Tuesday 11th

Mercury returns to your private zone and will continue to explore the depths of your shadow. Your mental abilities to process your feelings will be enhanced. Think of this time as searching for the gold you hid long ago. It's time to shine and heal old wounds. Be gentle with yourself during this time.

Wednesday 12th

A partner might help to put some pieces of the puzzle together today. You could be using them as a sounding board, but be careful not to express any negative feelings which have nothing to do with them. An emotional roller-coaster could take you for a ride through several areas of life.

Thursday 13th

Although you may be prepared to go as deep as you dare to find answers, you might have too many options which can confuse you. Try to stick to one track and follow that one through before jumping on another. Your first piece of gold is waiting to be discovered today.

Friday 14th

Your mental energy is highly active today. This is great news for your personal work, but not so great if your family or social groups distract you. However, you are learning how to love and forgive yourself more. Your inner child may need some reassurance and encouragement.

Saturday 15th

Keep up the good work searching your soul, but spare some time to treat yourself. This evening you may be staying in your safety zone as you've had enough excitement for one day. If others try to coax you out, stick to your guns and let them know you're safe and happy.

Sunday 16th

A passing phase could be challenging. It would help if you comforted yourself with what you love to do. This may involve travel documentaries or cooking exotic foods. Nurture both your body and soul. Contemplate what home means to you and protect yourself from invaders of your time.

Monday 17th

Work or other activity might make you feel vulnerable. You could choose one close friend or relative to talk to and let off steam in a safe place. Be kind to yourself and know that this process is showing how courageous you are. Get back in touch with your creativity.

Tuesday 18th

A powerhouse lights up your darkest corners. If you stay positive, alert and on task, you could have a revelation. You might also be so empowered that people take notice of what you have to say. Be an example for others to follow. This is your hidden gold showing up.

Wednesday 19th

You may have to be brutal today and lay the law down about something you're not happy about. However, you can put this across well enough not to cause friction. Stand your ground if you're confronted about this. Don't let others push you around or make you small again.

Thursday 20th

You are becoming a force to be reckoned with. This is evident today in the way you handle situations at work. You might also be rearranging finances and getting more control. This might not be easy, but with perseverance, you can solve any issues. Unwind with friends and interest groups this evening.

Friday 21st

Today is more easy-going and you can relax. You could be contemplating your relationship and what it is that you share with each other. This could be finances or shared pleasures. Look at this methodically and practically without letting emotions guide you.

Saturday 22nd

Something from your psyche could push its way to the surface today. This could make you feel exposed but can also be a cause for celebration. You may be surprised by how important this is to your self-esteem and wish you'd revealed this talent or dream a long time ago.

Sunday 23rd

Saturn turns direct now, and you may notice the pressure from family members is eased. Perhaps you've set strong boundaries this year and people have more respect for you. You may also have a stronger resolve to take care of your own needs better. The Sun moves into your sign. Happy Birthday!

Monday 24th

A general sense of satisfaction fills you. Your heart and head are in sync and you might feel more in line with your inner compass than previously. Not only do you know your limits and have identified where you push yourself too far, but others have realised this too.

Tuesday 25th

A new moon in your own sign lets you set goals and intentions around you and you alone. Venus has entered your sign too and can enhance the need to think about your values, self-worth and how you attract beauty and quality into your life. If you want more of this, make a wish.

Wednesday 26th

Today might feel a little edgy after the last few days, but this only serves to make you more determined to stick to your convictions. A family member may try to push your buttons and a partner could be asking for trouble. Deal with this knowledgeably.

Thursday 27th

Stay alert for something else coming up from your psyche. It might be small but no less significant to your personal growth. You could be pushing the boat out and being impulsive today, so take care with your spending as it could easily get out of hand. Only do what's necessary.

Friday 28th

Jupiter jumps back into your romantic and creative zone. Is there something you didn't finish earlier this year? Perhaps you have loose ends that need tying up or a forgotten project waiting in the cupboard. Now is your chance to complete this or to make a grand gesture to a lover.

Saturday 29th

Mercury is done digging for gold. It's up to you now to bring it forth yourself. If you wish to take a break from this personal journey, do so knowing you have the tools to pick it back up in the future. Your spider senses are tingling and desire some intrigue.

Sunday 30th

Your ruler, Mars, turns retrograde today. This period might be the excuse you need not to push ahead with deep and mysterious topics. If you really must pick up a new project, start from the very beginning and use the guidebook. Take it slowly and master it.

Monday 31st

You could be optimistic today, but an air of anticipation hangs over you. This is due to your understanding that shifts are happening and you're not sure if you have control. Keep an open mind and think outside the box. Perhaps your old ways of doing things need a total overhaul.

NOVEMBER
. . . .

Tuesday 1st

Today is definitely not the day to push ahead. You could be experiencing many triggers from childhood which fill you with self-doubt. This heavy energy suggests that you need to take time to gather your thought and resources. Which limits are self-induced, and which can you break through?

Wednesday 2nd

You may be overthinking and getting yourself in knots today. Your physical and mental energy aren't co-operating. Move your focus onto your romantic and creative projects and let out anything you have bottled inside. Old loves and hurts may return to your awareness. Let them go and unburden yourself of this baggage.

Thursday 3rd

Your emotions and deep thinking can be your saving grace today. As your mood lifts you can process thoughts in your own unique way. Think and feel from the heart and you can be more productive and turn overthinking into self-analysis. Remember to be kind to yourself during this process.

Friday 4th

Hold on to your inner compass today. You could be creating something which is unusual for you and will need to play around with it for a while. The perfectionist in you might be critical, but the romantic keeps you working until you're satisfied. Don't rush your work, master it.

Saturday 5th

You might have a better idea of what you need to throw in the cosmic waste bin today. This can come as a revelation and can also bring some heartache. Don't project this trauma. However, it's essential that you release this in order to move on and be your best self.

Sunday 6th

A day with the family could be good. There may be a lot of jobs that need doing and a group effort would be effective. You could be leading the way and organising this. Tricky discussions involving the past could occur and these must be concluded, forgiven and forgotten.

Monday 7th

If you feel like indulging with good food and company, make sure that all your daily chores are completed first. You could be more selfish now and wish to do your own thing, but you will come up against a problem if you neglect your duties. Do the responsible thing then have fun.

Tuesday 8th

A full moon and lunar eclipse in your relationship zone could throw a spotlight on what you've achieved. The strange energy can be disturbing and throw you off balance. Listen to your inner voice and refrain from reacting in old unhelpful ways.

Wednesday 9th

Watch what you say today, volatile energy can mean that you speak without thinking. There may be issues of jealousy or nastiness within your relationships. You can turn this energy into something more exciting if you play it right. Decision making may be difficult later on, so take time to consider all the options.

Thursday 10th

You may have to be humble and turn to someone in your family for advice. This might also be an overdue apology. Something isn't fitting right at the moment and you need to get to the bottom of it. Try not to be fooled into wishful thinking or false romantic notions.

Friday 11th

Burning the candle at both ends will only make your health suffer. You might notice this today as your energy wanes and you have trouble doing menial tasks. Your mental processes may be preoccupied with things that aren't important right now. Slow down, rest and prioritise.

Saturday 12th

Listen to what your inner voice is telling you as it's possible that it is communicating with your true north and checking if you're aligned. You might feel out of sync and could do with some nurturing to get back on track. Consider where you feel most protected and why you refuse to allow this for yourself.

Sunday 13th

You might be more sensitive and intuitive today. Use this wisely as you can navigate your way through the day with care and empathy for others. If you feel safe, you can relax and help others to feel the same. Do what feeds your soul and give yourself a treat.

Monday 14th

Stay in your safety zone this morning and come back to that feeling if you feel attacked or vulnerable. What you hide from others is your softer side, but sometimes you need to expose this so you can be appreciated and understood. Find your voice this afternoon and be a leader.

Tuesday 15th

Beware of illusions today. You may have been under the impression that romance and creative pursuits were going well. This may be possible, but there is also a risk that you get drawn into idealistic thinking. Check in with your core values and keep a level head on your shoulders.

Wednesday 16th

The planetary energy suggests that you shift your focus from yourself to your value system. Think about your goals and aspirations. What resources do you have? How can you gather more of what you need? It might be time to restructure your home, finances and personal philosophies.

Thursday 17th

Your friendships may need your services now. You could be in demand or going through a sorting process and deciding which contacts no longer serve your best interests. Be part of a community or group who believe in the same things as you. Don't give your time to those who don't share your values.

Friday 18th

Practical work will be good for you now. Filing, sorting, making lists and joining in social activities can be helpful. You might have to put your personal dreams and introspection to one side and contribute to a group venture or a good cause. Shake up the system and start a revolution.

Saturday 19th

A quiet weekend is favoured as you might need to process recent events alone. Put your creative projects aside and simply put your personal world to rights. You can get a better idea of what means the most to you now if you use compassion and research.

Sunday 20th

You might not have the time or energy to blend in with the crowd today. If you need to decline an invitation, do so politely and offer them your services for another time. Alternatively, you may be interested in connecting with elders and discussing family history to piece together missing information.

Monday 21st

There may be something urgent to do today. This could involve putting yourself out there to be noticed. Perhaps you've overlooked a deadline or appointment. As the Moon returns to your sign you may feel this intensely. Express your desires this evening. Be honest and open-minded.

Tuesday 22nd

A brief moment of nostalgia or a yearning for past times must be dismissed as this can bring your mood down. It can also induce problems and arguments in your current relationship. Look ahead at what new things you can achieve with the one you love. Aim high and stay sharply focused.

Wednesday 23rd

If you can connect to your inner compass today, do so as a reality check. However, it may still be evading you. Practical, hard work might be an alternative answer. Intense feelings can make you super productive, but this can also exhaust you.

Thursday 24th

Jupiter turning direct and a new moon asks that you seek truth in everything you do. Look at the quality in your life. What holds value for you? What is too materialistic? Perhaps you need to indulge yourself with connecting to the wider world and exploring more. You may be attracted to other cultures and higher education.

Friday 25th

You might need to slow down and use today for minor adjustments. It's possible that there's been a shift and you need to catch up with it. If you hate change, this can be troublesome. Learn to embrace the ebb and flow of what life has to offer.

Saturday 26th

A day of reflection could be good for you. The festive season is about to kick off and you may be too busy for this. Today you might be able to connect to your partner around finances and shared investments. You could be thinking of change with too much emotional attachment.

Sunday 27th

Reconnect with people you've neglected recently. You could win some brownie points if you reach out to a lover and rebuild your relationship. It may have been a tough few months, but you have a chance now to get back on track and co-create a harmonious life together.

Monday 28th

You could be slogging away today at your responsibilities and feel like you're getting nowhere. All you can do is to forge ahead and lower your expectations of yourself. No one is asking for a miracle, just that things get done and deadlines are met. Don't stress too much about this.

Tuesday 29th

Mentally you may be drained today. Unfortunately, you must soldier on until you've completed your work. You may need to be around someone close this evening to let off steam. Find a friend who won't be offended if you speak openly and honestly about your grievances. Let it all out and then breathe deeply.

Wednesday 30th

Let yourself drift today. You could feel lighter after offloading your baggage. Going with the flow can be easier and less of a problem. You may feel that you're a small fish in a big sea, but this doesn't bother you today. A simple day is what you need.

DECEMBER

· · · · · · · · · · · · · · · · · ·

Thursday 1st

Don't let anything rock your boat today. You might be adrift and switching off, but outside influences continue to nag at you. Hold onto your inner compass, but remember that not all is as it seems right now. Stay calm and centred and let the outside world pass you by.

Friday 2nd

You may be more optimistic today and can come back to mundane life with a smile on your face. This break might have boosted your health and strengthened your constitution for the upcoming festive season. Do what's necessary and look forward to a weekend with exciting plans.

Saturday 3rd

It's likely that you're extra busy now and can breeze through your day with strong motivation. You might be inspired to spend on luxury goods or connect with others from far away. Reach out to people you have neglected lately and plan for an evening of swapping stories.

Sunday 4th

Neptune turns direct now. You could begin to see things more clearly and get an upgrade in your artistic and romantic endeavours. Be careful that you aren't clinging on to a dream that wasn't meant for you in the first place. Let it go and seek a new perspective. Partners can be supportive now.

Monday 5th

Put your best foot forward and extend your gratitude to someone special. You may not have the chance again. Big projects may be coming to completion and you should feel proud of yourself as this might give you a place in the wider community. Excitement or restlessness fuels you.

Tuesday 6th

You deserve the good things in life. If they're offered today, grab them with both hands. This could mean a jump start to get your dreams manifested. Your emotions may run deep but your mind can be more grounded and help to anchor you. This is a great starting point for adventure.

Wednesday 7th

Enjoy a day free of difficult energy. You may be returning to your deep and personal inner work, but remember that your ruler, Mars, is still retrograde in this section, so lower your expectations and take things slowly. Look around, survey the territory and learn what you're dealing with.

Thursday 8th

A full moon highlights what has been going on for you regarding shared investments, learning, teaching and researching. Financial matters could come to a head and may need urgent attention. You may also have a revelation regarding your inner workings and the darker corners of your psyche.

Friday 9th

You may feel insecure today and could do with gentle chats and words of encouragement. Look to maternal figures who can offer this and take extra time to listen to what they say. Your emotions may be larger than usual, and your concerns could be out of proportion. Let yourself be looked after today.

Saturday 10th

Loving words and harmonious communication can be a source of comfort today. You might realise that the long road of personal development is never-ending but worth every step. Commit yourself to undertake this quest and make it your goal to be kind to yourself along the way.

Sunday 11th

If you begin to feel vulnerable or exposed today, look at your achievements this year. Someone needs to tell you that you've worked extremely hard and have accomplished a lot to be proud of. Come out of the shadows and shine. Let yourself be seen and heard because you are worthy of success.

Monday 12th

It could be time to reach out to family members and offer them gratitude for their support this year. You may also be seeing the bigger picture and be thankful for the lessons you've learned about maintaining healthy boundaries. Group ventures and family matters can also be celebrated.

Tuesday 13th

Some irritation is possible today, but you must refrain from using selfish or boorish behaviour to get your own way. This phase will pass, and you must respect that others have their own stresses to deal with too. Use up your restless energy in another way such as exercise or planning.

Wednesday 14th

Today you could be the go-to person for your social activities. As you're good at organising, you may be called upon to host an event which can be fun and adventurous. Put pen to paper and brainstorm your ideas now. You can be imaginative but practical at the same time.

Thursday 15th

Great earth energy can ground your ideas and help them to grow. These may be short or long-term and you don't have to hurry to meet deadlines. Surprise yourself by setting a pace that you're unfamiliar with and be guided by it. This can be much slower than you're normally used to.

Friday 16th

You could be ignoring your personal dreams today as what you're doing for the moment is more important and time-consuming. This doesn't mean that your own agenda is forgotten about, it simply means that you are prioritising what needs to be done. Reconcile this to yourself later.

Saturday 17th

You may have a conflict of interests now and a pang of regret that your own path has been side-lined. Don't worry too much about this. Use your mental energy to get through the next few weeks. Surprise someone special with an unexpected phone call or message this evening.

Sunday 18th

Balance your own needs with those of your family unit today. There may be jobs to do or plans to be made with your tribe. This might interfere with your rest time and you might need to withdraw if it gets too much. Stay in control as tempers could flare up today.

Monday 19th

The Moon in your sign intensifies the atmosphere and insists that you put every effort into being your best self now. This could mean that you've let things slide a little or put your energy into what's not so important. Hard work and dedication will make the day go quicker.

Tuesday 20th

Jupiter bounces back into your health and duties zone. This can be a great sign for your health, but as he expands everything he touches, you must remember not to take on too many responsibilities. If you must, then try to have fun with them.

Wednesday 21st

The winter solstice arrives with the shortest day. This could make you feel rushed to get your workload done. However, you should pause, reflect and reward yourself for the past year. This evening you might wish to switch off and snuggle into the winter nights ahead.

Thursday 22nd

Your one-to-one relationships might need attention today. Expect the unexpected and you may have a lovely surprise. Try to involve family members in the planning for the festive season. Don't take it all upon yourself. You could easily get emotionally overwhelmed, become unfocused and make mistakes. Ask for help or delegate duties.

Friday 23rd

A new moon in your communication zone can help to make your mind up about what you wish to pursue for the coming year. This is likely to include study, research or networking with others. It can also be something which will take a lot of time and energy.

Saturday 24th

Today the air is filled with anticipation. There may be many messages or visits to make before bedtime. However, there should be no hiccups as the planetary energy is favourable and even romantic. Your words and desires match your deeds and you can create beauty in anything that you do today.

Sunday 25th

Your family life is blessed with love, altruism and humanistic attitudes today. Prepare yourself for a fun-filled day with much joy and laughter. However, you could overdo the good things, so be careful. Your tribe may pull together to make this a truly great day to remember.

Monday 26th

You may need to relax today and not do very much at all. It could be that you indulged too much yesterday and are regretting it today. You should lie low and do as little as possible. Show the younger members of the family what it takes to be responsible and respectful.

Tuesday 27th

Today you can relax more and do your own thing. You may not have too many duties to do and can drift off into your own fantasy world. If you choose to spend time with a lover, you may have a dreamy time and be reminded of your shared visions for the future.

Wednesday 28th

There are blessings available for you if you know where to look. These may be your sense of adventure and willingness to try new things. Your inner compass calls you and if you check in, you might see that a compassionate way of communicating is winning you bonus points.

Thursday 29th

Mercury turns retrograde today. Just as the year ends you are reminded to back up devices, double check travel plans and be more mindful with your speaking and listening. You could feel an instant effect of this today and you will need to be extra careful with your planning.

Friday 30th

Tiredness could set in today, so don't do anything over and above the necessary. You may have some thoughts about your personal path, but now isn't the time to pursue this, so keep it on the back burner until after the holidays are over. Make plans in your head for next year.

Saturday 31st

There is a lot of challenging energy around today. You could be rebelling against your duties or suffering with your health. Either way, you may not be in the mood to party. You may wish for something more intimate with a loved one.

Scorpio

....

PEOPLE WHO SHARE
YOUR SIGN

PEOPLE WHO SHARE YOUR SIGN

· · · · · · · · · · · · · · · · · ·

Scorpios have seduced our screens for decades, from Scarlett Johansson to Goldie Hawn, so it's no wonder that they have a reputation for being the sexiest sign in the zodiac calendar. The Scorpion is a mysterious creature that has brought dark depths to the world in the form of Martin Scorsese's films, and wonders of entertainment in the form of RuPaul's Drag Race. Discover which of these intriguing Scorpios share your exact birthday and see if you can spot the similarities.

24th October

Shenae Grimes (1989), Eliza Taylor (1989), Drake (1986), Wayne Rooney (1985), Katie McGrath (1983), Roman Abramovich (1966), Malcolm Turnbull, Australian Prime Minister (1954), Kevin Kline (1947)

25th October

Rylan Clark-Neal (1988), Ciara (1985), Katy Perry (1984), Craig Robinson (1971), David Furnish (1962), Chad Smith (1961), Pablo Picasso (1881), Johann Strauss II (1825)

26th October

Seth MacFarlane (1973), Phaedra Parks (1973), Tom Cavanagh (1968), Keith Urban (1967), Uhuru Kenyatta, Kenyan President (1961), Dylan McDermott (1961), Rita Wilson (1956), Hillary Clinton (1947), Jaclyn Smith (1945)

27th October

Kelly Osbourne (1984), Marla Maples (1963), Simon Le Bon (1958), Luiz Inácio Lula da Silva, Brazilian President (1945), John Cleese (1939), Sylvia Plath (1932), Roy Lichtenstein (1923), Theodore Roosevelt, U.S. President (1858)

28th October

Frank Ocean (1987), Troian Bellisario (1985), Matt Smith (1982), Joaquin Phoenix (1974), Julia Roberts (1967), Matt Drudge (1966), Bill Gates (1955), Caitlyn Jenner (1949)

29th October

Tove Lo (1987), Ben Foster (1980), Tracee Ellis Ross (1972), Gabrielle Union (1972), Winona Ryder (1971), Rufus Sewell (1967), Kate Jackson (1948), Richard Dreyfuss (1947)

30th October

Janel Parrish (1988), Clémence Poésy (1982), Ivanka Trump (1981), Matthew Morrison (1978), Nia Long (1970), Gavin Rossdale (1965), Diego Maradona (1960), Timothy B. Schmit (1947), Henry Winkler (1945)

31st October

Willow Smith (2000), Frank Iero (1981), Piper Perabo (1976),Vanilla Ice (1967), Rob Schneider (1963), Peter Jackson (1961), John Candy (1950), Zaha Hadid (1950), Michael Landon (1936), Carlos Drummond de Andrade (1902), Sardar Patel (1875)

· · · · · · · · · · · · · · · · ·

1st November

Penn Badgley (1986), Aishwarya Rai (1973), Jenny McCarthy (1972), Jeremy Hunt (1966), Anthony Kiedis (1962), Tim Cook (1960), David Foster (1949), Larry Flynt (1942)

2nd November

Nelly (1974), Stevie J (1971), David Schwimmer (1966), Shahrukh Khan (1965), Warren G. Harding, U.S. President (1865), James Knox Polk, U.S. President (1795), Marie Antionette (1755)

3rd November

Kendall Jenner (1995), Colin Kaepernick (1987), Gabe Newell (1962), Dolph Lundgren (1957), Kate Capshaw (1953), Larry Holmes (1949), Anna Wintour (1949)

4th November

Jessa Seewald (1992), Dez Bryant (1988), Guy Martin (1981), Bethenny Frankel (1970), P. Diddy (1969), Matthew McConaughey (1969), Ralph Macchio (1961), Kathy Griffin (1960)

5th November

Virat Kohli (1988), Kevin Jonas (1987), Alexa Chung (1983), Luke Hemsworth (1981), Danniella Westbrook (1973), Famke Janssen (1964), Tilda Swinton (1960), Bryan Adams (1959), Kris Jenner (1955)

6th November

Kris Wu (1990), Emma Stone (1988), Conchita Wurst (1988), Taryn Manning (1978), Thandie Newton (1972), Rebecca Romijn (1972), Ethan Hawke (1970), Kelly Rutherford (1968), Mohamed Hadid (1948), Sally Field (1946)

7th November

Lorde (1996), Bethany Mota (1995), David de Gea (1990), Elsa Hosk (1988), David Guetta (1967), Joni Mitchell (1943), Albert Camus (1913), Marie Curie (1867)

8th November

Jasmine Thompson (2000), Lauren Alaina (1994), Jessica Lowndes (1988), Erica Mena (1987) Tara Reid (1975), Tech N9ne (1971), Gordon Ramsay (1966), Bonnie Raitt (1949), Alain Delon (1935)

9th November

French Montana (1984), Caroline Flack (1979), Nick Lachey (1973), Eric Dane (1972), Lou Ferrigno (1951), Carl Sagan (1934), Hedy Lamarr (1914), Muhammad Iqbal (1877)

10th November

Mackenzie Foy (2000), Kiernan Shipka (1999), Zoey Deutch (1994), Taron Egerton (1989), Josh Peck (1986), Miranda Lambert (1983), Diplo (1978), Eve (1978), Brittany Murphy (1977), Ellen Pompeo (1969), Hugh Bonneville (1963), Neil Gaiman (1960)

11th November

Tye Sheridan (1996), Vinny Guadagnino (1987), Philipp Lahm (1983), Leonardo DiCaprio (1974), Calista Flockhart (1964), Demi Moore (1962), Stanley Tucci (1960), Kurt Vonnegut (1922), Fyodor Dostoevsky (1821)

12th November

Anne Hathaway (1982), Ryan Gosling (1980), Gustaf Skarsgård (1980), Tonya Harding (1970), Nadia Comăneci (1961), Megan Mullally (1958), Hassan Rouhani, Iranian President (1948), Neil Young (1945), Grace Kelly (1929)

13th November

Matt Bennett (1991), Devon Bostick (1991), Gerard Butler (1969), Jimmy Kimmel (1967), Steve Zahn (1967), Whoopi Goldberg (1955), Chris Noth (1954), Frances Conroy (1953), Andrés Manuel López Obrador, Mexican President-elect (1953), Robert Louis Stevenson (1850)

14th November

Russell Tovey (1981), Olga Kurylenko (1979), Travis Barker (1975), Gary Vaynerchuk (1975), Josh Duhamel (1972), Patrick Warburton (1964), Charles, Prince of Wales (1948), Astrid Lindgren (1907), Claude Monet (1840)

15th November

Paulo Dybala (1993), Shailene Woodley (1991), B.o.B (1988), Sania Mirza (1986), Lily Aldridge (1985), Jeffree Star (1985), Chad Kroeger (1974), Jonny Lee Miller (1972), Jimmy Choo (1948)

16th November

Pete Davidson (1993), Vicky Pattison (1987), Gemma Atkinson (1984), Maggie Gyllenhaal (1977), Paul Scholes (1974), Brandi Glanville (1972), Missi Pyle (1972), Lisa Bonet (1967), Sheree Zampino (1967)

17th November

Tom Ellis (1978), Rachel McAdams (1978), Lorraine Pascale (1972), Jeff Buckley (1966), Jonathan Ross (1960), RuPaul (1960), Danny DeVito (1944), Lauren Hutton (1943), Martin Scorsese (1942)

18th November

Nick Bateman (1986), Fabolous (1977), Anthony McPartlin (1975), Chloë Sevigny (1974), Owen Wilson (1968), Kirk Hammett (1962), Elizabeth Perkins (1960), Kim Wilde (1960), Linda Evans (1942)

19th November

Tyga (1989), Adam Driver (1983), Jack Dorsey (1976), Jodie Foster (1962), Meg Ryan (1961), Allison Janney (1959), Charlie Kaufman (1958), Calvin Klein (1942), Larry King (1933), Indira Gandhi, Indian Prime Minister (1917)

20th November

Michael Clifford (1995), Oliver Sykes (1986), Future (1983), Andrea Riseborough (1981), Kimberley Walsh (1981), Ming-Na Wen (1963), Sean Young (1959), Bo Derek (1956), Joe Walsh (1947)

21st November

Conor Maynard (1992), Colleen Ballinger (1986), Carly Rae Jepsen (1985), Jena Malone (1984), Nikki Bella (1983), Ken Block (1967), Björk (1965), Nicollette Sheridan (1963), Goldie Hawn (1945), René Magritte (1898)

22nd November

Hailey Baldwin (1996), Alden Ehrenreich (1989), Scarlett Johansson (1984), Boris Becker (1967), Mark Ruffalo (1967), Mads Mikkelsen (1965), Jamie Lee Curtis (1958), Rodney Dangerfield (1921)